TOO BUSY TO BE HAPPY

Too Busy to Be Happy

USING EMOTIONAL REAL ESTATE TO GROW *YOUR* WORK-LIFE WISDOM

CHRISTINE LAPERRIERE

LIONCREST
PUBLISHING

TOO BUSY TO BE HAPPY
Using Emotional Real Estate to Grow Your Work-Life Wisdom

ISBN   978-1-5445-0169-7 *Paperback*
          978-1-5445-0170-3 *Ebook*

I dedicate this book to my two amazing children, Catrina and Xander. This book houses the tools and practices I am committed to using in my effort to be the absolute best mom I can be.

Contents

Part Three: Bringing Concepts into Practice

Introduction

You wanna fly, you got to give up the shit that weighs you down.

—TONI MORRISON

Years back, I was asked to teach a course on "Mastering Me" to a large group of managers and executives. The man leading the rollout of the program had decided that this was the right title for the course, even though I struggled to understand what "Mastering Me" meant. To prepare for that event, I spent a lot of time in my office trying to dig through my expertise to figure out what I'd actually mastered. What was I an expert on that I could teach in the form of a course?

I'd spent seven years in engineering school—I survived years of undergraduate and master's level calculus. I had been a vehicle design engineer for one of the big three American automotive companies, which made me the envy of most men at every dinner party I attended. I had worked in management consulting, which had helped me build business acumen to build trust, help clients, and win repeat business. I had started my own consulting firm, and I was becoming well-known for my work helping teams reach a higher level of performance. From the outside looking in, I'd mastered a great deal. But what wisdom did I really have to share? They too were full of similar lists of flashy accomplishments. The only thing that I felt was a real, unique accomplishment was a skill I had never prepared to learn—it was how to manage my stress and finally conquer my vicious battle with burnout.

It's important to know that I'm an expert in being busy. For the majority of my life, I was especially amazing at being too busy to be happy. My lifestyle of busyness had ultimately led to burnout, then years more spent healing and learning all I could in order to recover. I'd wanted to figure out how to be both busy *and* happy. And today I can say I've made great gains in this area thanks to the framework of emotional real estate. Although I worried people would leave that course feeling they wanted their money back, I took a risk and taught the course around that framework, to help people create mastery around work-life wisdom. I wanted them to know how to bring more happiness back into their busy lives.

Although I tossed and turned the night before the

course, to my surprise, the audience—a roomful of high-achieving women—loved it.

On each break and after class, person after person came up to me to thank me and tell me they finally understood what was happening in their lives. I must have had twenty-five people tell me their life story—how they felt like they couldn't keep up with the successful lives they had created. So many shared how their stress levels were high and balance was hard, and how they felt they were being smothered by their to-do list. Women who I'd been intimidated by—who looked like they had it all together—would tell me, "Oh my God, the same thing is happening to me." Like me, they'd spent hours in courses and conferences just like this one, where they were taught sales and communication and all sorts of tactical things, but never how to manage stress. This is one of the biggest problems we all share. How do we manage it all?

Robert Epstein, PhD, of the American Institute for Behavioral Research and Technology, surveyed 3,000 people on stress and its effects. In that study, he found that 25 percent of happiness hinges on how well you handle stress.* Yet *no one* is talking to us about this thing that we've all lost sleep over at night, and we see the repercussions everywhere. This is why there's a huge market

---

* https://www.everydayhealth.com/womens-health/physical-side-of-stress.aspx,
http://drrobertepstein.com/

for pharmaceuticals to manage stress and stress-related illness. It's why so many people these days struggle with depression and sometimes turn to drug and alcohol abuse. It's why we're frustrated at work and in our homes—the feeling of stress is directly connected to our feelings of happiness (or lack thereof).

I'd struck a chord. I started to teach this content regularly. And so many times, I ran into people at restaurants or events who would remind me that I'd taught their Mastering Me course. They would thank me, and they'd repeat that phrase over and over again—emotional real estate. They would tell me about how they shared it with their sister, their friend, their husband, and how they felt it should be a standard part of education for everyone. People told me they were making decisions differently so that they could allocate their energy more consciously. They asked where they could read more about it. It was like magic. I was onto something that not only changed my life but could really help other people.

So, as we embark on this journey together, I want to start by asking you a question: are you too busy to be happy?

When you hear people talking about work-life balance as though there's a perfect formula for "having it all," do you ever catch yourself thinking, *Yeah, right?!*

Balance implies, first of all, that work and then life are a 50/50 split. And that there are only these two elements to the whole. And striving for the ideal concept of balance makes us think, incorrectly, that achieving that ideal will make us happy all the time. After all, if you can manage to give exactly half of yourself to your kids, husband, work, and an attempt at a social life, why *wouldn't* you be happy?

But you and I both know it's not that simple. Balance feels less like a shifting scale and more like spinning plates. And if you are like me, you're tired of stepping over broken glass.

Here's the real kicker: even when your schedule is impossibly crowded, the busyness is not actually the crux of the problem. It's the guilt. It's feeling like there's not enough time to devote to what really matters. It's being mad at yourself when you procrastinate on the things you'd like to focus on. It's how you keep saying, "I should do that"—how you keep "shoulding" all over yourself. *I should exercise more, I should eat better, I should get to the gym, I should read more books, I should do that course.* It's the dusty DVD cases or video downloads filled with infomercial-sourced yoga classes that you're convinced you'll get around to when you have more time. The things you keep around because you're sure you've just been too lazy to get to it and that, one day, you'll be able to.

If you find yourself too busy to be happy, you have a bigger issue to deal with than balance. In fact, the struggle for balance creates a mental dizziness, where you're always counterbalancing and shifting the load from one side to the other. You have committed yourself (your *full* self) to more things than you can sufficiently pay attention to. We understand this with time and with money. We know there are only so many hours in the day and dollars in the bank. Sometimes we can borrow time from sleep hours or run up a credit card bill, and we know we'll eventually have to pay back the debt. But when it comes to energy and focus, we tend to overspend without a second thought. And the debt piles up, but it's less obvious to see—the quality of our relationships suffer, the quality of our health suffers, and ultimately, if unattended, we feel our soul being sucked dry.

This is stress. It's when the perceived workload is greater than the perceived resources to get that work done. And if we continue to borrow in the form of stress, the consequences can range from missed small moments to unrepairable damage to our health, relationships, and career.

Everyone gets stressed, though I've found that men seem to stay very goal-oriented and laser-focused, able to compartmentalize to experience stress in different ways. Women, on the other hand, tend to take on seventeen different things and try to keep them all moving at once. When we're helping out at the bake sale for one daughter, we're also preparing for the board meeting, thinking about whether the other daughter has her gear for swim day tomorrow, and planning to grab a present for a coworker's birthday later that week. It's a mental game that many of us feel like we can't stop playing. From the stay-at-home mom to the high-powered professional, a reel of high-pressure self-talk spreads our focus around to everything that's happening, all at once, and we convince ourselves that it's all at the same priority level. It's an unsustainable way to pursue an unattainable goal, yet so many of us keep trying anyway.

Believe me, I know. In the next couple of chapters, I'm going to tell you about how I allowed stress to start to eat away at my life and how heavy the burnout became. The good news is that you don't have to reach that same level of burnout to want to shed work-life *balance* and instead pursue work-life *wisdom*.

HAVING THE WISDOM TO STOP THE BALANCING ACT

Tell me if any of this seems familiar to you. It used to be that even when I was seriously overbooked, I'd still add one more thing to the calendar. I felt like I needed to keep adding one more thing and one more thing in order to keep up with it all. Did I have an hour of downtime? I should listen to three chapters of a self-help audiobook!

Half an hour in the car driving home? That's the perfect time to (over)think about a conversation I'd had with a teammate and further justify what I said in that meeting. Forty-five minutes on the treadmill? A chance to consider how to rethink that failing project. Mentally, I did not rest. Even if I was eating ice cream and watching Netflix, inside I was plotting a path to my next big goal. If I was not busy or stressed to some degree, I felt that something was missing. I assumed that I wasn't living up to my fullest potential unless every second was filled, so I never let my mind be quiet. That attitude kept me relentlessly busy and, ultimately, unhappy.

I devoured volume after volume in trying to work out how I became too busy to be happy. Maybe this isn't the first book you've read on this topic, either. And while I appreciated the common theme among these authors—slow down, try yoga, practice meditation—I could never make space for any of their advice. Meditation seemed particularly ridiculous. Spending what I assumed to be hours doing nothing at all was the enemy of everything I had become attached to. I recoiled at the thought of sitting still or slowing my mind down. I felt unimportant when I didn't have something important to think about. So, if none of the best books had the answer, how could I find this coveted "balance" I'd heard so much about?

When you're too busy to be happy, there's a feeling

of being out of control. Whether it's a calendar that's constantly full or mental clutter that doesn't ever slow down, choosing happiness and finding time for yourself seems impossible.

At peak busyness, I felt like I was on a treadmill that kept going faster, and it was all I could do to just not fall off. Like Lucille Ball at the candy factory, I was grabbing everything that was going by me, stuffing it in my pockets, eating all that I could, never managing to catch up. What I didn't know was that I could slow down the machine. That's the thing about busyness—it's reactive. Everything seems to be happening *to* you, and you have to respond to it.

The concept of balance implies that if you don't have everything exactly where it should be, you'll fall or fail. The treadmill will keep running, and you'll either have to keep up until you burn out or get off entirely. Work-life wisdom, on the other hand, allows us to optimize our energy—to become empowered to get back in the driver's seat of our own lives.

Instead of aiming for balance and delicately tipping the scales from side to side, work-life wisdom can create the space we need to be both happy *and* busy. While work-life balance demands us to fill our schedules out with enough pieces of the pie for everyone and everything, work-life wisdom allows us to move through the day to the rhythm of our priorities in the moment, paired with our strengths and our passions.

Work-life wisdom is noticing when you've missed two dinners in a row at home and you are aching to see your kids—announcing itself like gears grinding in a car when you haven't shifted in time. It's becoming attuned to what your life looks like when it's running smoothly and knowing when you need to make some adjustments. It's creating priorities and making active decisions to stay present in the moments that make up your life. It's asking ourselves not only if we have enough time or money to do something, but if we have enough energy—enough emotional real estate.

Work-life wisdom is empowerment to finally break the cycle of busyness. In this book, I want you to learn what boundaries look and feel like and realize that setting them can help you become empowered to make decisions in your life once more. You don't have to settle. You can learn to manage your life rather than reacting to the way life seems to batter you around.

Learning to negotiate work-life wisdom requires more than writing a new to-do list. It requires you to take on an entirely different perspective—to learn a new language. I call this language "emotional real estate," and it's one I want you to be fluent in by the end of this book.

Through the framework of emotional real estate, I've found and created reliable tools and practices that have helped not only me but so many of my clients navigate our busy lives without succumbing to them. There's a huge win waiting for us when we learn to employ work-life wisdom effectively in our lives. On the other side of emotional real estate, there's genuine enjoyment of our busy, modern lives. It's how we can stop to smell the roses, in real time.

WHAT TO EXPECT IN THE PAGES AHEAD

Whoever you are and whatever your story, I want you to know now that the paradigm of emotional real estate can help you make decisions, negotiate conflict, manage change, do away with baggage from the past, and handle baggage that's already filling up for the future. I want you to know that you can develop an awareness of what your emotional real estate looks like and become empowered to make choices that help you manage your energy wisely.

If you feel like you can't find the time to be happy, I hope this tool kit will help you create that space in your life again. If you feel yourself nearing burnout and want to prevent it, I hope these tools keep you from hitting bottom. If you're rebuilding your life, I hope to teach you to see what you're doing right so that you can keep doing it intentionally. I say "hope," because this book is not for people who just want to think about these ideas once; this book is for people who know that progress comes with practice. Make these concepts a practice, and I hope one day you'll look back at pictures thinking of them much like the "before" shots from that new body makeover advertisement you just saw on Facebook. You'll look in the mirror at the "after" shot of yourself looking stronger and happier, lifting those heavy weights with confidence.

I've learned these lessons the hard way, and I'm going to challenge the habits you've formed over many years— habits that have served you in some way and will be difficult to let go. In these pages, I'll help you understand what a system of stress looks like and learn to identify those danger zones. You will begin to notice when you're succumbing to circumstances and slipping into old habits, and you'll have the tools to stop the spiral before it begins. I think of it as constant forward momentum; if happiness exists on a scale of one to ten, managing your emotional real estate helps you to move ever closer to ten on the scale every day.

In part one, I'm going to get real with you and take you on my journey through burnout and recovery. This is not some idyllic dream about a balanced life or a one-size-fits-all prescription to add to your growing list of obligations. I've lived the journey to the bottom, and I can share the concepts and tools that I used to find my way back out.

In part two, I'm going to share with you critical concepts you need to understand. If you just want the meat, head right to this section. Read and re-read these so you feel completely up to speed with these simple but useful concepts.

In part three, once you have a working knowledge of the language of emotional real estate, we'll be able to get into the specifics of those tools. One by one, we'll walk through the habits and perspectives that are littering your emotional real estate, then the tools that you need to clear them.

By the end of the book, you'll not only have a new context for decision making, but you'll have a tool kit full of practical habits, exercises, mindsets, and routines ready and at your disposal. I could simply offer up this new perspective—an infrastructure for work-life wisdom based on what I have learned. But I hope you'll get more out of this book than just lessons and speeches. I encourage you to sit down with a pen and paper, think each concept and tool through thoroughly, and then put them to practice. Reach out to your friends, coworkers, or mentors to start the conversation about emotional real estate with them. Work through these tools side by side. Share the language of emotional real estate with others who can encourage you along your way. Support each other as you regain control and rediscover how to create more happiness.

With the right mindset and a good set of tools, you can be both busy *and* happy. I promise.

Part One

My Story

CHAPTER ONE

Workaholics Anonymous

I have a theory that burnout is about resentment. And you beat it by knowing what it is you're giving up that makes you resentful.

—MARISSA MAYER

Health is not just about what you are eating. It's also about what you're thinking and saying.

—PENNY PHANG

I've always been driven to succeed. For a long time, my high-performance personality seemed to be one of my biggest strengths. Most who worked with me saw me as ambitious and very hard working. After I finished my undergrad and master's degrees, I started my career in engineering with one of the major American automotive companies—my dream job.

After a few years, I wanted to take on a bigger challenge, so they sent me into manufacturing. When that wasn't enough, I left that position for a boutique management consulting firm. Within a few weeks on the job, they promoted me into my first leadership role. Now I had people reporting to me, I was living in a swanky condo in downtown Toronto, and I was driving a red Mercedes. I had created the life of my dreams. My life was all about the big job, big city, fancy car, cocktails with friends, business travel all over North America, and the freedom to take luxury vacations.

So why, then—even on my "good" days—did I not feel happy?

For years, I was highly motivated to keep climbing the ladder, and I liked that about myself. I enjoyed working hard, and I always believed that with hard work I could make anything happen. I hadn't gotten here by mistake; I had envisioned the life I wanted and made it happen. But still, I didn't feel happy.

TOO BUSY TO LOOK BACK

This wasn't the first time I'd been an overachiever without really knowing if I was happy. Looking back, I've always been a multitasker. In high school, I participated in theater, sports, and music while running my own manicuring business and taking advanced math and science classes. It was the same in college. I was the first female project manager for the Formula Society for Automotive Engineers team, building a race car to compete against other schools from around the world. Oh, and did I mention part-time tutoring, a busy social life, and a boyfriend? I was constantly juggling extracurriculars, finishing a big project, or setting a new goal.

When I was studying for my master's degree, my grandmother was spending her last days in the hospital. To ensure I didn't cut my workday short, I would head in before 7:00 a.m. to make up for the lunch hours I'd spend with her, then come home late to study for my courses even later into the night. I was a master at staying on the fast-moving treadmill, although it came with occasional consequences. I remember one time waking up to an excruciating toothache, which turned out to be a molar that I'd cracked while grinding my teeth in my sleep after studying until three in the morning for an exam.

I thought that better scheduling would make it all work. We only have twenty-four hours in a day, and I wanted to make the most of every single one of them. So instead of feeling motivated by my to-do list, I would dwell on a mental "didn't get it done" list. From the second I left the office, I felt guilty about the dozens of things left on my plate. If I didn't get every single thing done, I'd spend time beating myself up for not being disciplined enough. Once, I remember telling my boss, "I have seventy-four things on my to-do list this week," and I wasn't exaggerating. It was impossible, but I thought that if I could just be better, I *could* get all those things done. Looking back, it's amazing how much mental busyness we can create for ourselves.

In addition to my busyness, I struggled to get clarity on decisions. I was always trying to analyze my relationships, wondering "should I stay, or should I go?" None of my decisions could just *be*—they had to be carefully and perpetually analyzed. It was a mindset of constant mental strain, debating whether that relationship was right, or this comment meant something more or how this other thing was frustrating. The smallest things, if we stew on them long enough, become a huge burden that we can't even lift anymore, let alone get rid of it. I carried so much baggage from my past and expectations for my future that it felt like trying to live in the past and the future at the same time. I wouldn't let anything go. My inner critic was loud and had silenced my inner champion.

TOO BUSY TO BREATHE

So back to feeling unhappy. Through hard work in consulting, I'd just been voted manager of the year and awarded another promotion with a larger team and more responsibility—my first recognizable award for leadership, and a clear career high. Ironically, the night of our company event and the same night that I won that award, my long-term relationship crumbled before my eyes. Within a few days, I was in the middle of an unexpected and painful breakup, while my expectations at work were greater than ever. I started traveling every week, using planes, trains, and automobiles to get from task to task and team to team. Sunday nights were filled with dread. Monday morning, I'd wake at 4:00 a.m. to be packed and on a 6:00 a.m. flight to Newark, New Jersey, and make it home late on Thursday after hours of travel delays. On Fridays and through the weekend, I would lead a local project team in Toronto and get caught up on everything that didn't get finished through the week. I opened up my laptop in the morning and usually didn't close it until late into the evening. Each time a new task came across my plate, I'd take it on, and the creep of depression was edging in.

I lost interest in the things that normally made me feel alive. My sense of humor, my love for people, my creativity—it all started to fade away. I'm naturally extroverted and love people, but eventually I lost my passion for all the things I once knew. I knew I was depressed, so one weekend, in an effort to fire myself up again, I decided to go to a Tony Robbins event. As someone who has a love for inspirational speakers and the energy of big events, I figured it would be just the ticket. Within an hour after the event started, Tony Robbins asked us to turn to the person next to us and start a conversation. For some reason, this simple task felt like it was too much. I didn't want to talk to people—I just wanted to be left alone. I didn't have the energy to deal with that kind of thing, and I got up and walked out.

I had ambitions for life outside of work, too, but by the end of the day, I didn't feel like doing anything. I stopped exercising. I didn't feel like reading my inspirational books. I didn't feel like doing anything at all. There were so many commitments I couldn't manage to keep—calling my mom or my best friend, taking care of myself—but all I could do was sleep until it was time to get up and do it all over again.

Oh, and the inner critic was so loud! In my mind, I would constantly harp on all the ways I was weak, a failure, and simply not good enough. I felt like a complete and total fake—like someone was going to find out that this outward success had been awarded to the wrong person. I kept thinking over and over again about how I was completely failing at my job, failing at relationships, and failing at life. I never shared these thoughts—I kept it all to myself, like a dirty little secret.

No one in my company could know that I wasn't holding

it together, especially after I'd been promoted and had people looking up to me and reporting to me. This was my dream life—exactly what I'd wanted and built. The last thing I could show was vulnerability. I was sure that they would find out that I wasn't smart enough or good enough to be in that position. They'd see the weaknesses I constantly told myself that I had and would stop listening to me. That's what I told myself, anyway. But eventually, the inward stress appeared in outward forms.

I started to have strange physical symptoms that I was not well. In the rare moments when I did have a chance to catch my breath, I found that I physically couldn't do it. In meetings, on the plane, at home—no matter what I was doing, I couldn't seem to get a full, deep breath of air. It felt like someone had placed a stack of books on my chest. It seemed to get worse at times, where I'd just keep reaching for a deep breath. After my morning flight on Monday, I'd check into my hotel room early and just lie on the bed for a few minutes, trying to catch a breath before heading to my client's office for my meetings for the day.

When that feeling would grow the strongest, I'd focus on my lungs and pull in as much air as I could, only to still feel like I couldn't get enough air, or enough release. Outwardly, this sounded like a deep, audible sigh. Over and over again, I'd heave these deep breaths into sighs, to the point where people would assume I was simply irritated or impatient with them. It wasn't uncommon for people I worked with to suddenly backpedal on a point they were making or ask me why I disagreed with them—meanwhile, I realized that I had taken a big, huge sigh and they assumed my body language was telling them I was not in agreement. In reality, I was paying more attention to breathing than I was to what they were saying. My body was aching to breathe, and I was trying to—as I was working or running to catch a plane.

I was sure this signaled something wrong with my body, so I spent any downtime I had at doctors' appointments. I did sleep apnea tests, allergy tests, chest X-rays, stress tests, and echocardiograms. Test after test attempted to uncover why I couldn't catch my breath. After completing the exhausting list, my doctor said, "We've looked at everything, and I feel incredibly confident that your breathing problem is stress-related."

He scribbled out a note for me, tore off the piece of paper, and set it in my hand. "Here. This is a prescription for Ativan. Provided you have a high-stress job, I think this should help." I asked him if he had any other suggestions on how to lower my stress levels so I could breathe again. He shrugged—not really. I asked when I should stop taking Ativan, and he basically said I should plan to take it on an ongoing basis as long as I suffered from stress and the medication was helping.

That couldn't be right. There I was, a young and healthy single woman, holding a prescription for a drug to help me cope with my everyday life because the stress of it was taking away my breath.

What do you do when you can't handle the life you created for yourself?

You keep living it, of course. Or keep trying, anyway. I never filled the prescription. I still flew back and forth to New Jersey. I still lay in the hotel room and tried to breathe. I still worked longer than everyone, ate out alone, and went to bed to do it all again the next day.

I continued to dread Sunday nights. Sunday nights meant I had five whole days ahead of me before I could catch my breath again. I measured out the week, so I'd feel like I was making progress. On Tuesday, 40 percent of my week was over. Wednesday at lunch I was halfway through. Thursday meant cocktail hour because, thank God, we're 80 percent of the way there. Those two tiny days of weekend were not enough. If I lost half a day doing laundry or running errands, I'd mourn the loss of perfectly good weekend time that should have been spent relaxing.

Every morning, I'd drag myself out of bed, make myself pull it together in the shower, then put on my makeup—

mascara last—before leaving for work. As the days wore on, it became harder and harder to get out of bed. It became harder to pull it together in the shower. I'd lift the mascara wand and feel the tears start to come. It was more than mascara—it was the last step before walking out the door, and it completely overwhelmed me.

After weeks of tearing up as I applied my mascara, I remember finally feeling I couldn't take it anymore. As I lay there in the hotel room, staring up at the ceiling, thinking about the day ahead and how impossible it felt, I thought about how I just needed a break. Not a short break. I'd had long weekends and time off here and there, and it just didn't cut it. Maybe a week, but then I knew I would come back and soon I would be just as tired and miserable.

The longer the hypothetical break became in my mind, the more impossible it felt. There was no way I could leave the office for two or three weeks. And even if I could, it was not enough of a break. No one would understand. I was convinced of it. There was no way for anyone to understand just how badly I needed this time off. I felt like they'd see me as weak and unable to handle my job. I'd have to admit that I was truly a fake—not nearly as full of potential as they had all once thought. That I couldn't actually handle these things that everyone else did to be successful.

If only I could take a break—and have permission from everyone to take that break. If only they would feel I was brave or tough, not weak. I wanted to be forgiven for not being able to keep up with the stress of it all anymore.

Maybe if I was sick...like really sick. I could get a break, and no one would judge me. People would feel bad for me and give me permission to take care of myself. Really sick. Like, cancer sick.

Holy shit.

Looking back, this is absolutely what I consider to be my darkest moment. I'd literally had the thought that cancer would be the only way to slam on the brakes and catch my breath. The expectations I put on myself, along with my need for permission and justification from others, was so great that I was willing to let my mind go to some heavy, dark places. The thing is, I believed (and still do believe) so strongly in the power of the mind, that I realized how grave my situation was. I was pushing my body so hard and stretching my mind so thin that if I kept it up, I was most likely going to get very sick.

Let's be real here. If you're so low that getting cancer looks like a solution to any problem, your mental health is in dire straits. Diagnosed or not, my mind was sick. And while it's true that mental health is largely invisible and rarely valued by our employers, peers, and often ourselves—I needed to attend to mine, STAT. I'd hit peak burnout, and the only permission that I needed to take a break was my own.

CHAPTER TWO

Eat, Pray, Breathe

I've never seen any life transformation that didn't begin with the person in question finally getting sick of their own bullshit.

—ELIZABETH GILBERT

On my birthday, still struggling to breathe most days and in desperate need of a break, a friend gave me a copy of Elizabeth Gilbert's memoir, *Eat, Pray, Love*. I can still vividly remember this ridiculously cliché moment in my life—sitting in a hotel room, all alone, laughing and crying as I read these life-changing travels through Italy, India, and Bali.

In the book, Gilbert talks about how her secret stress left her on her knees, begging for something to be different. Like many of us, to the average person, her life didn't look that bad, but inside, she was melting. Oh, how well

I understood. With each new page, I couldn't help but think, *Maybe I can just walk away for a while?*

After another few rough weeks, I finally got the courage to do what I needed to do. I went to my boss and straight-out told him I was going to take an eight-week leave of absence, unpaid.

He said, "What if I don't want you to take a leave of absence?"

"Then I'll have to quit," I said, with more confidence than I had intended.

"Well, then I guess you're taking a leave of absence," he said, unimpressed but willing to oblige.

Although that might sound like empowerment, it was more like apathetically throwing my hands up. At that level of burnout, I was so tired and checked out that I just didn't have a choice anymore. Turning off completely was all I could do in the name of self-preservation.

Although I had gotten the thumbs-up to take a leave, my brain was still working on giving me permission to not care, whether or not my boss or my team or my clients were disappointed. I knew they were; a lot of them felt like I had a ton of work to do that summer, and I was ditching the team too soon. A few people suggested it was a career-limiting move. For the first time in my life, I felt I needed to hold my ground in honor of my own sanity. I was finally starting to prioritize my health and sanity over what others thought of me and my fear of a derailed career. My own self-care felt like the most important thing to me, and no one else had to validate my decision. I was finally willing to risk upsetting someone else in an effort to honor myself.

The next call that I made was to my best friend. I told her what I had done and also shared with her my plan to begin my break by renting an apartment for a month in Rome. I knew it had to be more than just a vacation. I needed this to be big, and I asked her if she wanted to come with me, at least for a little bit. It wasn't long before she had booked a ticket to join me.

In the weeks ahead, I worked harder than ever to get my projects and team ready to run without me. That put even more pressure on me than before, and although I was still feeling burnt out, the thought of getting away gave me the small boost I needed to push through.

PLEASE POWER DOWN FOR TAKEOFF

I remember boarding the plane to Italy in a complete daze, without any idea what it would be like to be away from work for two whole months. No emails to answer, no fires to put out, nothing to do.

The silence on the plane was overwhelming. I asked the flight attendant for a cocktail. And then another. And another...

After a long, drunken snooze on the flight, I woke up in Rome, ready to meet up with my best friend who was arriving on a separate flight, and before long, we set out for our first adventures in Rome.

The first week in Rome, I still felt lost a bit. It felt so strange to change gears. But thanks to my best friend, we ate, we drank, we did the tourist things, and most importantly, we laughed. We explored, we walked more, and again, we laughed—and laughed and laughed some more. I remember so clearly how the muscles in my cheeks ached each day as they had gone months without use. I realized I'd completely forgotten that I *loved* to laugh!

By the second week, I started to feel like I was on vacation. Relaxed and enjoying each moment, I felt like I was starting to get in touch with my inner wisdom, and I felt more connected with my body. Many days, I didn't feel like doing much but simply sleeping in, sitting in a gorgeous piazza with a cup of frothy cappuccino and those tiny little biscotti. I would put on my dark sunglasses so

I could secretly people-watch without letting anyone else in on my secret. I would stare at the pigeons playing around the statues in the center of the piazza and wonder if they knew what a beautiful place they lived in.

Week three, after sending my best friend back home with lots of pictures and fun stories to tell, I spent time enjoying the city alone. That said, it was interesting how much my mind struggled to let go of having a "to-do" list each day or something specific to accomplish. This bothered me. To spend a day feeling that I had not "made good use of my time." I had to allow days to go by where nothing interesting happened. That seemed crazy, especially in Italy—how could I not make this trip worth my while? If I slept in and only made it to the café at noon, I would think, *You wasted a good day in Italy. What's wrong with you?!* Each day, I had to make peace with the idea that if I was mindfully enjoying the moment, that alone was enough.

After meeting friends and making new friends along the way, by week four, I finally felt fully healed—as if someone had taken a tiny surgical instrument deep inside my brain and mended each little synapse and connection that was no longer firing properly. I felt full of life—really alive and full of energy. I found that I could just walk around—present, relaxed, and happy with a quiet mind. My sarcastic sense of humor returned. I loved sitting in a café and chatting with strangers. I loved wandering to the train station to accidentally land in Tuscany for the day. When a waiter brought me a plate of food with fresh basil and bright red tomatoes on it, I savored every sensation in attempt to lock that moment into memory forever. I didn't realize how broken my brain had become until everything started gluing itself back together again. It had been so long since I had felt worry or fear, my brain had acclimated to a much happier new normal. Oh, and I realized how much I love hanging out with just me! I'm actually a fun person to be around (says me!).

To my surprise, after the first four weeks of what felt like pure bliss and healing, I woke up starting to feel restless. And something else caught me by surprise: my breathing problems were gone. I'm not sure when I could finally breathe fully each day, but it dawned on me that somehow that weight on my chest that fought me for each breath had been lifted.

ITALIANS DON'T UNDERSTAND STRESS

Just to be clear, it wasn't just the time away from my old life that let me recalibrate. The Italian culture is something different entirely. They don't spend their days rushing from task to task. One night, early in the trip, a couple of Italian men asked me and my friend if we wanted to go out to dinner with them at their family restaurant. Their English was pretty good, and their accents were adorable. We agreed to have dinner with them—how could we not?

It was a picture-perfect night in Rome.

The summer evening was warm with clear skies, and we were sitting on the patio of a beautiful little family-owned restaurant, wine flowing, with amazing food and entertaining company. As the night went on and the stars came out, one of the Italian men asked me what brought me to Italy.

I told him, "I've been so stressed out. I have a very stressful job working extremely crazy hours. It turned into this health issue where I couldn't breathe, and my doctor says this health issue is due to stress."

I could tell by the way he was looking at me that he was checking out of my story a bit. He wasn't sure what to think. He leaned over to his buddy, and they chatted in Italian for a little second, while he kept looking back at me.

Finally, he said, "I'm sorry. I don't understand this word... *stress.*"

Now, I don't know whether there's really no word for stress in the Italian language or if he was just charming me, but he was clearly struggling to understand my story.

Either way, all of a sudden, I had chills up my arms as a huge aha moment hit me: I'd been using the word "stress" as a blanket statement to describe everything that was happening in my life and to explain who I was. In a way, using this word like this kept me from genuinely taking a close look and ownership for what was going on. In American society, we use stress as a convenient tag to describe so many things. How many people in your life have health problems that are simply labeled "stress-related?" We just tag it and move on. Can't sleep at night, can't breathe? It's just stress. If the doctor asks if you're under a lot of stress, you say, "Well, of course." Aren't we all? And my favorite, when friends and family hear your woes, they say, "You shouldn't stress so much."

That was a pivotal moment for me. I started to wonder: What if I took that word out of my vocabulary? What if I were no longer able to use stress as an identifier for myself? I realized that taking the word *stress* out of my vocabulary would force me to look much deeper at what actually went into that concept. I made a conscious decision that night to stop using the word stress to describe myself, an ailment, or how I was feeling. I would have to be clear—from now on, I would have to articulate how I was feeling, such as I'm struggling to make a decision, I fear I'm being judged, or I fear that people won't be happy.

If stress is simply a term to describe the difference

between *what you feel you have on your plate* versus *what you think you can actually handle,* then let's start talking about closing that gap rather than labelling ourselves by it.

COMING HOME

When I left for Italy, I wasn't sure how I would feel as the trip came to an end. I'd gone to Italy prepared for anything. I would have been perfectly okay with meeting a man and getting married and living in a Tuscan villa in the middle of nowhere for the rest of my life. I didn't care whether I made it back to work, and I hadn't promised to. But by week five or six, I was feeling ready to work again. I wanted to reconnect with the ambitious part of me.

As suddenly as relaxation had set in, the desire to work reemerged. I didn't want to let go of the parts of me that knew how to be at peace, but I didn't want to deny my ambitious instinct either. Instead, I wanted to invite the part of me that loves to make things happen back in and protect the happy and healthy place I'd found. I like to call this place my "True North"—it's the feeling I have when I'm passionately pursuing my work in a healthy and soulful way. I was ready to dive back into my career and add my ambition back into the mix to see whether I could move forward without losing touch with that True North I had just discovered.

STARTING TO STRESS LESS

Burnout, as I would discover over time, had been a huge gift. It gave me the biggest opportunity for growth that I've ever had, because I absolutely had to get clear and change my life in order to stop it. Time and time again, I keep finding that the size of the struggle you experience equals the size of the insight you have afterwards.

After my burnout and recovery, I began studying everything I could about how the mind works and how to harness it to improve our lives. I revisited lessons of spirituality. In less than five years after this experience, I had acquired a practitioner certification in neuro-linguistic programming, a year-long psychotherapy for professional certification, and a year-long intensive transformative coaching certification which required fifty hours of practice coaching and numerous trips to LA. I had spent almost as much as most people spend on an Ivy League MBA on my custom curriculum focused on human behavior, creating change, and ultimately, a deep dive into the nature of the human mind.

AS NLP (NEURO-LINGUISTIC PROGRAMMING) EXPERTS WOULD SAY...

The first thing I studied after coming home from Italy was neuro-linguistic programming. An approach to communication and personal development, NLP is the study of the conscious and subconscious mind and how the two work together. It looks at the connection between neurological processes, language, and behavior—all of which are affected by experience or by programming. Specifically, NLP examines language patterns that influence the way our minds consciously and unconsciously processes information.

NLP taught me how to sort through my thoughts and reframe anxious inner dialogue. It taught me to visualize the next right step and to prepare myself to take it. It also gave me clear and specific tools such as mind mapping, which I still use all the time with my clients and in my own life as part of the concept of emotional real estate.

Little did I know that, while I was being trained in NLP, I was about to become a living testament to prove that it works. In each weekend workshop, I was challenged to bring my own problems to the table as practice. We often started with visualization exercises—*focus on something you want to create*—so I regularly pictured starting my own business...in five years.

My teacher kept reminding me, "The subconscious mind can't picture five years." The subconscious mind cannot understand time. The same way you can't picture an elephant in five years, your brain only knows how to picture the elephant or not. That meant I could only picture *start-*

ing a business or *not starting* a business. I told my teacher I understood, but that I didn't want to start a business right away. I was sure I wasn't ready. I knew I wanted to wait five years.

I finished the NLP course mid-June, and only a few short weeks later—without a lot of thought and fully aware of how ridiculous it was—I told my boss, "I'm giving you my three-months' notice. I'm quitting, and I'm going to start my own business."

Like taking a big giant leap off a cliff without a safety net to protect my fall, it was not the perfect time. I hadn't checked off all the boxes that I believed needed to be checked in order for me to start that business. I hadn't even established any savings. But I'd done an excellent job programming my mind to effortlessly put one foot in front of the other to move forward with my dream. Incidentally, I had also eliminated all the obstacles in my head that kept me from starting my own business. I reached out to a company with an amazing sales and methodology training—at the time known as Miller Heiman—and asked them how I could start my business by selling and delivering their sales methodologies. Within a few short months, I was in business for myself. Danger alert: this is what happens when you set your mind to something!

AS THERAPISTS WOULD SAY...

As exciting as I found these tools, I became skeptical about the practice of reframing every negative thought by changing the language and energy around it. I didn't think that was always possible, or even healthy. Something was missing. I wanted to understand the deeper layers that keep people stuck. How do you deal with childhood trauma, deep sadness, anger, and disappointment that feels rooted in years of history?

I soon decided to pursue a certification in Gestalt psychotherapy. Gestalt therapy appealed to me because it meets people in the present moment, while deeply considering the context of a person's life and experience to date. The key insight of Gestalt is that the context of the individual's experience matters. When people have a chance to go back and visit the past and see it through a current lens, oftentimes they can move forward with less sadness, anger, and painful emotion. That said, as I finished my one-year certification, I felt hungry to spend time supporting people on strategies for the future and less time digging into challenges of the past.

AS TRANSFORMATIVE COACHES WOULD SAY...

As I learned about each type of therapy, I saw their strengths, weaknesses, and values, and I found concepts from NLP and Gestalt psychotherapy useful, but I knew there was more out there. Less than a year after being immersed in the principles of Gestalt, I discovered a life coach named Michael Neill. Together with six or seven of his favorite coaching teachers, Michael built a curriculum based on "the three principles" (invented by Syd Banks) called *transformative coaching*. The method was profoundly different from anything else out there, because it taught people to become present and at peace with the truths that already existed. Transformative coaching revolves around understanding the way the mind, consciousness, and thought work together to create our human experience.

Remember those stereograms or three-dimensional pictures that seemed to be everywhere in the 1990s? The posters and pictures were made of little jumbled dots and, at first glance, they looked like just some colors on a page. You couldn't see the "hidden" images unless you stood at just the right angle and looked through the picture. Suddenly, there'd be an eagle flying out at you. And once you saw that eagle, you couldn't un-see it. It had been there all along—you just needed to focus correctly in order to spot it.

Transformative coaching works the same way.

Think of it as climbing under the hood and taking a close look at how your mind works. One thing you'll notice, if you really shine a light in there, is that the ups and downs we all experience are normal. Nothing is permanent. You might be in a bad mood right now, but one day you'll be in a good mood again. It's the nature of the mind to be constantly changing. Keep looking and you will see that thoughts can trigger responses that shift your mood. You might be completely happy right now, but if I told you a story about a post I read yesterday that was tagged "#metoo," I could bring your mood right back down again. Our response to thoughts dictates our feeling in the moment.

Transformative coaching is a constant analysis, assessment, and awareness of what you are feeling. The shifting state of the mind is a central premise. Instead of fighting our feelings, we learn to allow the shifts, so we have less of an internal battle and more peace with what surrounds us. One thing we learned with confidence is that our experience of life is an inside job and not reflective of what is happening around us.

Transformative coaching was absolutely, literally transformative for me and my interactions with clients. Still, I was frustrated by the way the model could sometimes oversimplify life. Oftentimes we would hear, "It's just a thought," but I wanted to know how exactly to untangle this spaghetti of life that kept piling onto my plate. As I worked with clients, I began to see that NLP, Gestalt therapy, and transformative coaching each had an important role to play. Together, these three concepts could help build resilience. But I kept feeling the influence of some earlier learnings that were constantly niggling at me.

AS KABBALISTS WOULD SAY...

All along my journey, I was passionate about finding how spirituality fit into this equation. I thought back to 2005, when a small Kabbalah store down the street from my condo had captured my attention. I walked past it every day, and eventually my curiosity got me in the door. Kabbalah is Jewish mysticism, dating back thousands of years. Their teachings focus on karma and the movement of energy. For example, they talk about the energy of money and how it moves around the world. They talk about the energy of people and karma. Kabbalah resonated with me and provided a framework for letting things go.

A key concept of Kabbalah is that there are two opposing forces of energy. One is connection to ego or self, and the other is connection to light or the creator. Any given person at any given time feels called to both sources. This opposition is constantly in play, with you in the middle trying to figure out which calling to follow.

Our culture encourages us to lean toward the ego side. Think about modern businesses, or the industrialized world itself: our entire environment is wired to create for the sake of self. When I was in consulting, I wanted a promotion because it would lead to a more prestigious title and more money for me. That's ego. And suffering seems to follow you when you're chasing things that only benefit your ego. When I'm struggling to let something go, I now find it's almost always something connected to ego. As soon as I realize something is connected to my ego alone, I know it's something I need to let go or to re-approach.

Over time, when I began to shift my attention toward serving more people and creating a bigger impact on the world, I had a different perspective. Looking through the lens of light, I saw everything around me more clearly.

When you're connected to light or the desire to receive for the sake of others, every decision becomes simpler.

Like the thoughts that we allow to come and then let go, awareness of these connections to ego can help us move through drama faster. When your energy is spent serving your family and friends and growing a business that helps people, you can see that direct line from your energy to helping others as a result. When you're disappointed that your Facebook post didn't get as many likes as you thought it should, it pings as ego, and although the ego would like to start a fight in your mind, you can move right along. Thinking this way provides a compass for deciding how to direct your energy and has helped me find my True North more than once.

AS BUDDHISTS WOULD SAY...

After I studied Kabbalah for quite a few years, I discovered two Buddhist centers in Toronto and started to take classes there, too. In the Buddhist centers, they dedicate space to the important practice of meditation. They take you to a room, sit you down on pillows, close the door, light the incense, and leave you there for fifteen minutes. Fifteen minutes may not seem like much, but it takes a lot of work to shut everything off. The group setting helped me stay disciplined when I normally wanted to ditch this practice after just three minutes on my own.

Often, we think of meditation as having no thoughts at all. So when it gets quiet and you suddenly can't think of anything but the burger you ate for lunch, you *try* to get rid of the thought. *Why am I thinking about this now? Why can't I just get quiet?!* Then you manage to get rid of that thought, and the next minute later, a dog barks. *They shouldn't allow dogs barking in the city. I'm trying to meditate! What's wrong with the city—someone should hand out tickets for noise pollution!*

Thoughts are okay—the brain does crazy things when it's trying to get quiet. With practice, you can allow the thoughts to come and go like slides on a projector screen while you separate from the busyness and the trying.

I learned to become aware of what Buddhists call the "monkey mind." Those thoughts are going to come and go, and when you understand the way the mind works, you don't get so worked up about them. It's just doing the busy things that the mind does. Eventually, you learn to stop identifying the thoughts at all. You can separate from your mind a bit, allowing it to be busy *doing* without feeling like you have to pay attention to it.

Early in my career, I couldn't even comprehend the value of sitting completely still in silence. Even when I was recovering from burnout in Italy, sitting perfectly still in a beautiful piazza, drinking a coffee, and watching the pigeons—I'd immediately get antsy and feel like I needed to be "doing something." I'd often pull out my journal and start strategizing about the future or coming up with a game plan for the day. Now, years later, I can appreciate that simply being present is a valuable way to spend time.

Full disclosure: I've never been able to create a "proper" meditation practice. My meditation practice is quite literally seven minutes a week (more in chapter five). I've had lots of intentions. New Year's resolutions, even. But I'm still practicing. The idea that you "need time" to meditate discourages many people from trying. Everyone I know *wants* to start a meditation practice, but they don't find the time for it. Later, we'll talk about the one-minute meditation that's been helpful for me as part of my morning routine. Sometimes that one minute of quiet is enough to remind you what it feels like to be mindful and present and what's possible when you are.

Mindfulness sounds weighty, but it just means bringing your conscious attention to your five senses, regardless of time. It's developing the ability to feel yourself—to move up in your head while rooting in the ground—to bring yourself back to the present moment.

Being present 100 percent of the time would be brilliant, but it's not always possible. Instead, I try to think of ways to practice presence as part of my day. I enjoy finding slices of time to slow down, pay attention, and catch my breath. In fact, mindfulness becomes a type of meditation itself.

When I'm on site with a company, facilitating twenty-four people through an intense strategy session on diversity and inclusion, sales growth, or leadership transformation, I can't sit in a corner and light my incense and sound my chimes, but this practice teaches us how to drop into mindfulness meditation within the moment. One of my favorite tools for cultivating mindfulness is walking meditation. Walking meditation invites you to take your meditative practice into your regular movements. Any time you can integrate meditation into something you already do all the time, it becomes that much more accessible.

When I'm working and I walk to the corner for a cup of coffee, I've learned to drop into meditation on my way so I can quickly reenergize. When I drive, grab an Uber, or ride the subway downtown for a client engagement, I take that time very purposefully. I intentionally do nothing that isn't relaxing or returning emotional real estate. I often make sure I spent some portion of that time fully present and watching the people on the train. Then, when I get to the office, I feel like I have more presence and can start my day more effectively.

The magic of mindfulness is that I am making a conscious

choice to be in the moment and *know* that I'm not missing those moments even though I'm technically in the room. When I'm spending time with my children, for example, my mindfulness is heightened. I want the quality of those minutes to be high, so I want to be fully present in them. Sitting with my daughter in the evening, I'm conscious of being mindful, like taking time to enjoy that warm stream of water in my morning shower. I can honestly say, thankfully, if I were to die tomorrow, I would feel like I *experienced* the connection with my kids and the *feeling* of motherhood.

AS MY TEACHERS WOULD SAY...

A word to some teachers who were missed here: during this time, I spent a lot of time reading, listening, and talking to many wise souls. Among them are Louise Hay, whose work on affirmations and energy work continues to inspire me; Wayne Dyer, whose teachings on spirituality and the Tao Te Ching completely inspired me to be my best; Byron Katie, who calls on us to appreciate the present moment without judgment; Steve Chandler, a coach who taught me the concept of owner and victim mentalities; Rich Litvin, whose high-integrity, no-BS approach was always been a "Hell Yes!" for me; Brené Brown, who granted me permission to forgive myself for my imperfections (the very long list of them); and Nancy Kline, who taught me about creating space for others to have "time to think" so they can access their own inner wisdom to solve their problems.

WHEN YOU KNOW BETTER, YOU DO BETTER

What I've taken from all of this knowledge is a way of life that is in contrast to the way I used to live. As much as I appreciate everything I've learned and all the teachers I've encountered, I've never been able to maintain unwavering loyalty to one point of view. I don't think I could have studied one of these modalities to the exclusion of the others. It's taken each one of them to teach me something vital to contribute to the paradigm of emotional real estate.

I felt a little like Goldilocks with the porridge—it took some work to find things that were just right. The more I learned, the more the concept of emotional real estate came to light. Elements of each of these lessons and concepts became the building blocks from which I would create the paradigm that changed my life, my clients' lives, and hopefully, yours as well.

Ultimately, the breadth of my study has allowed me to be creative with the ways that I coach, mentor, and help people and businesses, as well. I don't want to be—I don't want *you* to be—limited by the shortcomings of any single perspective. The system that you're about to learn incorporates the most potent lessons from each perspective that has shaped my life and my interactions with clients. It's how I came to operate with work-life wisdom, and it's time for us to dig in.

Part Two

Core Concepts

CHAPTER THREE

Emotional Real Estate

Everything you've been looking for—happiness, love, connection with your children, wealth, and freedom—is an inside job.

—PRASSANA TADI

We seem to be continually weaving elaborate conceptual webs around even straightforward events. We distort reality and shroud it with complications by superimposing fabricated mental constructs. This distortion invariably leads to mental states and behaviors that undermine our inner peace and that of others.

Having a simple mind is not the same as being simple-minded. Simplicity of mind is reflected in lucidity, inner strength, buoyancy, and a healthy contentment that withstands the tribulations of life with a light heart. Simplicity reveals the nature of the mind behind the veil of restless thoughts.

—HENRY THOREAU

So, after experiencing burnout and years of education to help me understand human behavior, I finally understood one concept very clearly: your mental, emotional, and physical energy are all finite, and they are inclusive of each other and connected to how you feel in each moment. Hence the term I've created, emotional real estate—the total amount of available energy you have in those three areas. In the past, I had always believed that I had unlimited amounts of mental, physical, and emotional energy, so I created the perfect environment for burnout to occur. The moment I finally grasped the concept that I had a fixed amount of emotional real estate, everything changed. I began to rethink the way I allocate energy, just as closely as I budget my time and money. When I think about devoting energy to something, I ask myself if it's a good investment.

Emotional real estate goes like this: picture your front yard. Your literal front yard, right outside the front door of your house. You can probably see a certain amount of space to plant trees and grass, to build a deck or a pathway, to have a sitting area or a garden. No matter how much you'd *like* to do in that yard, you've only got a finite amount of property available. You can use it any way you want to, as long as it fits in the space that belongs to you. That's your available real estate. It doesn't grow or shrink every day, but there's a lot that you can do to optimize it to make it something you enjoy. You have choices about what you can do with that space and how you can respond to things outside of your control, like the weather and nature.

It's the same in life. We all have a fixed amount of space available for our goals, activities, events, and creations. Our "property" gets filled up as we process change, drama, baggage, decisions, procrastination, and relationships. If we're dealing with stuff from the past, we're using emotional real estate. If we're dealing with a lot in the present moment, we're using emotional real estate. When we plan for the future, we're using emotional real estate.

Emotional real estate is simply a way to visualize the amount of focus and attention needed to attend to the thoughts that are swirling through your mind at any given moment, and the energy needed to maintain focus on the actions you need to take each day. Absolutely anything you are thinking about—mindfulness of the present moment along with the laundry list of thoughts, feelings, and emotions running in the background—is taking up some kind of space. Emotions are, too, because they are simply thoughts that have been brought into the body.

Things like baggage with your dad are very different from things like working on your PhD, of course, but they all take up space. Anything from physical actions to external tasks to triggered emotions can use up energy, and that energy is limited.

"I CAN'T BELIEVE I SNAPPED"

One day, a coaching client, Jane, called me to tell me she'd just broken down crying in a meeting. She was absolutely floored that she'd cried at work. In a string of self-sabotaging behavior and negative self-talk, she called herself weak, wondered what people thought, and didn't know where to go next. She said, "I can't believe I cried in a meeting. This is career suicide! I'm going to have to quit my job. I can't do this anymore."

As we started to talk about what happened, I asked her why she felt like she needed to quit her job. She said that she should have been stronger. She felt weak. She felt embarrassed, humiliated. She couldn't believe that she'd been so weak that she cried in a meeting.

"There was no reason to cry, really," she said. "One guy made a comment about my team, and I just lost it. Tears filled my eyes, I couldn't keep it together anymore, and I had to get up and excuse myself. Over one comment about my team!"

"Walk me back," I said. "Explain to me what has been going on for you over the last six weeks."

It all came pouring out. Her son had been sick for a month and in and out of the hospital as the doctors searched for what was wrong, and no one could figure it out. Her relationship with her mother was also under pressure as she was frustrated with the lack of support she was receiving when she felt she needed it most.

While Jane was out of the office a lot caring for her son, everything started to fall apart with her team. Infighting, arguments, and chaos reigned, and she wasn't there to manage any of it. When she walked into her first meeting after having spent a full week away in the hospital caring for her son, she found her team in all kinds of trouble, and one team member who she trusted might now need to be fired.

When these problems landed in her lap, she was still processing everything else going on in her life, guilt over being back at work while her son felt awful, and the strain the past few months had put on her family relationships. All it took to push her over the edge was one comment.

She felt embarrassed, but when we put the situation into perspective, she realized it was completely understandable that she had cried in a meeting. Of course she did! Her emotional real estate was so full, something had to spill over.

You may go along thinking, "I can do it all, as long as there are no surprises." But the surprises will come. Maybe you need to pay a $500 bill to replace the tire you just blew out on the expressway. Or your kid gets into a fight at school and you discover that he's been in a bit of trouble lately. If you had only a little bit of emotional real estate left, you'd use all that energy processing the new situation. If you didn't have any emotional real estate available before this new problem reared its head, you might feel ready to snap.

There is an incredible benefit to growing awareness around the state of our emotional real estate, and you'll start to know if you have some in reserve or if you're completely at max capacity. Think of monitoring your emotional real estate as like looking at the dashboard of your car. If you never look at the gas gauge, you'll be shocked when the tank runs dry and you sputter to a stop on the side of the road. Just like in your car, self-awareness acts as a gauge to help you keep track of what kind of energy you have in reserve. When you sit in the driver's seat and monitor those gauges, you won't be surprised by a low mood or an overpacked schedule—you'll see it coming.

Jane hadn't been evaluating her emotional real estate. She immediately blamed herself for the tears—she thought it showed she wasn't strong enough to handle one little criticism—rather than realizing she was out of resources.

So many of us do that. When I was on the way to burnout, I kept telling myself the story that I wasn't strong enough. But that wasn't the real problem for me any more than it was for Jane.

We weren't weak; we simply needed to have more emotional real estate at our disposal.

TAKING OFF THAT BADGE OF HONOR

If emotional real estate is the front yard, just beyond it is what's happening in the present moment. Whatever is filling up our emotional real estate stands between us and being present.

If you had nothing on your emotional real estate at all, you'd simply be fully 110 percent present each moment of each day without any thought of the past or future moments. Maybe you've had this experience for a few seconds when you tried out a new yoga class or when you were enjoying a moment in nature on a beautiful day. But we are looking at it from a broader perspective—not just moment by moment but day by day and week by week.

And if we're going to start cleaning up our front yard, we have to start paying attention to whether we've littered our lawn with trash on purpose...because it's addictive.

FINDERS KEEPERS

The term "emotional real estate" came to me from a most unexpected source: an executive I once worked with who was known for being verbally condescending and quite rude.

Okay, that was too polite. He was an asshole.

Many years ago, when I was managing a team, one of my team members, Julie, asked me to join a call with this executive as she was frustrated trying to get an issue resolved with him. As I listened in on the call, she told the executive, "This potential customer just called in. They've been trying hard to get ahold of you, and you haven't returned their call for three or four days. Now they're calling me over and over again, trying to understand where you've been."

With his thick, Texan drawl, he replied with quite an arrogant announcement: "Naw listen Jooo-leeee, I do nawt have the eee-motional reee-al estate to dee-al with this right now. Anything else ya'll wanna talk about?"

And that was it. He completely shut her down. I was simultaneously appalled—livid!—at his condescension in the face of a valid concern brought to him by another employee...and at the same time completely fascinated by the term I had never heard before.

This man was truly terrible with people internally and damaging as a team player, but what I observed was his laser-focused approach to what he needed to accomplish to benefit his own personal success. He was known for being excellent at sales and sales alone. All his energy, his emotional real estate, was funneled into a single, specific direction, and it allowed him to be successful even if he upset lots of other people along the way. As much as I wanted to reach through the phone and wring his neck, this one quick phone call really made me think.

So, I stole his term. Fair and square. And I don't use any emotional real estate feeling guilty about it.

The concept of stress has become almost a badge of honor in our society. I remember feeling like I had to work hard and look stressed or people wouldn't think I was really committed to my work. We have to break the belief that stress is the only way to get things done.

In our culture, that's often considered normal. The American Dream is available to us if we work really, really hard and set really, really big goals and never stop fighting for them, right? It seems to work for a while as you chase down every lead, and when they pay off is a big account or profitable investment. That's when many people begin to get addicted to the stress cycle. It can be incredibly challenging to separate stress from success in our minds, so if we're ambitious enough to expect success, we feel like we're being realistic to also expect stress to come with it.

Let's look at that expectation a little bit closer, though. Sometimes, if we're honest, juggling lots of things feels like validation that we're important. This sums it up for me:

We wear our stress like a badge of honor, humble-bragging about how little sleep we got last night, how our weekend was spent racing to meet a deadline, and how we're too busy to take a vacation. This lifestyle seems to have reached epidemic proportions, with 63 percent of Americans reporting feeling stressed and more than a quarter citing a "great deal" of stress, according to a spring 2014 survey by NPR and the Harvard School of Public Health. The majority of twenty-somethings and women credit the sheer weight of too many responsibilities as the source of their angst.*

We're so conditioned to expect to feel stress that clients regularly balk when I suggest they slow down a bit. They start by saying, "What am I supposed to do, just sit on the couch all day?" They find it almost offensive that I've suggested they shouldn't be stressed. And then the next layer is exposed. They tell me that if they weren't so busy, they would have to sit with just themselves and their thoughts, and they are intimidated by that idea. Busyness has been a distraction for them.

I wish I could tell you that creating this space is the pathway to enlightenment and that I've mastered it all completely. But the truth is, this awareness of your emotional real estate is a practice and not a destination. I'm still not able to be fully mindful and completely present in every single moment. More realistically, we're working toward creating *more* presence and *more* peacefulness in our lives, even though life is always going to be using up some amount of emotional real estate. When we learn to operate with free space, we retain our ability to become

---

* https://www.huffingtonpost.com/2014/08/19/stress-addiction_n_5689123.html

present, no matter what's happening around us. It's our way to be both busy and happy.

HOW RAISINS TEACH US MINDFULNESS

My first taste of mindfulness happened early on, while I was still a student in university, soon to graduate from engineering school. I was studying 24/7, trying to keep up with my friends and boyfriend, trying to exercise and eat right, and working two jobs. I worried about getting a job, about whether I was in the right field, and about whether I could hack it in the corporate world. Often, I lived on three or four hours of sleep and a few cans of Diet Coke.

A longtime friend of mind had just gotten his first job in Seattle and invited me to come for a visit. I was excited to see how life after school was treating him. On the plane, I was seated next to a curious lady wearing a knit hat and a long, multi-colored dress, carrying a purse made of various pieces of random fabric sewn together. I immediately tried to look busy, reading something or doing whatever I could to not make eye contact. Annoyingly, she still started to make small talk. She was insistent about it. *This was going to be a long plane ride.*

I learned that she was a professor in psychology for a university, and one of the courses she taught was mindfulness. She told me how rare it is for people to slow down enough to truly recognize a moment in time. She pulled a tiny box of raisins from her purse, handed me one, and told me to hold it.

"In my class," she said, "I start with raisins."

I felt really awkward, but I was in the window seat and couldn't get past her.

She told me, "I want you to experience it. What do you notice about it? What's interesting about it?" She wanted me to look at it. Feel it. Smell it. Use all my senses to experience the raisin. Then, she told me to put the raisin in my mouth. Yes, the raisin I had rolled around in my hand for ten minutes.

As I put the warm, fingered raisin in my mouth, she said, "I don't want you to chew it right away. Set it in your mouth, and again, notice what you're smelling. What you're tasting. What's the sensation? How does it feel on your tongue? After you've completely embraced that experience, then you can chew it. Notice what it feels like. When you finally bite into it, what sound does it make?"

So, there I was, very slowly eating a single raisin while the airplane lady talked about it, thinking, *This is the most bizarre plane ride I've ever had in my life.* Even so, she got me thinking. How often do we stop and study or observe what's going on? How often are we completely 100 percent focused on experiencing anything, let alone something simple? My brain only wanted to see my time used for productive things or planning for the future.

When I got off the plane, I was so inspired by this conversation with this eccentric woman that I made it a mission to stay present the whole weekend while I experienced this new city. I embraced it. I felt caught in the iconic moment of a rainy Seattle day. I ordered a latte and took the time to smell it, to pay attention to the first sip and really feel the foam. The experience. The feeling of being damp but cozy. Watching the people who came in and their mannerisms in conversation. I just *watched*—as a complete observer, without any judgment. I was fascinated with how each of my senses were engaged in the moment in front of me while I sipped a latte on a rainy day in Seattle.

That weekend, I sat with my friend on a bench under a windowsill of an impossibly cool old house, and we had wine, cheese, and crackers and talked about life. It can be hard for me to remember details from yesterday, but slowing down and savoring the moments of this trip stored those memories away differently in my brain. Although it has taken me years to practice mindfulness on a regular basis, it was on that plane with that woman and a single raisin that I realized just how rare it was for me to be present or mindful in my day-to-day life. That lesson would ultimately become a game-changer.

So often, we think we can just keep expanding to handle everything or cramming something new in. I know I did. But if we change those expectations—if we recognize there's only a certain amount of space available—then we have to start thinking about what can actually fit within those limits.

As soon as I give people the visual tool of emotional real estate, they can see how they've been filling it up and what they've left out. Only then can they think, *What has to be there and what can I let go?*

I often ask, "Think of one problem and picture it on your front lawn. What percentage of your emotional real estate is used up on it?" It could be a bad boss, a comment a family member made, or an impending decision. They're usually things that shouldn't take up a lot of space or energy, but they do anyway.

Most stressed clients often realize that they are using up more than 50 percent of their emotional real estate on one thing. Oftentimes I ask what they feel is important to them right now and should be getting more emotional real estate. Many times, what they are using their energy on versus what they care about most is not aligned.

So, here's the thing: if you only have a fixed amount, you can't go spending it on everything that knocks at your door—you have to get frugal with it. We're used to saying, "I don't have enough time," or "I don't have enough money" as reasons to say no, because we know that those things come in fixed amounts. We don't just give them away—we mindfully choose how to ration out what we have.

The first step to letting go and creating the space to be happy is to understand the capacity of energy that you have, and that it's just as finite as time and money. This is the key to understanding emotional real estate. As soon as you see energy as a limited resource, you become more frugal with it. If you're on a fixed income, you won't just blow it on anything. You get pickier with what you value and invest in, because you know the resources will run out sooner or later.

A UNIVERSAL FRAMEWORK FOR INDIVIDUAL LIVES

The fastest way to get your arms around the concept of emotional real estate is to sit down with a paper and pencil and map it out. First, check in with yourself and ask whether you're happy. Most of us answer the question with a "yes, but I could be happier if..." And if the answer is an obvious no, then this work becomes even more important. Visualize your front lawn filled with things that are devouring your emotional real estate. What's eating up your space? Where are you using up your emotional real estate?

I have sheets of paper filled with lists of everything using up my emotional real estate in a given moment. Sometimes it's a thought. Sometimes it's a feeling. Sometimes it's a commitment that I made that I'm feeling stressed about. To get a handle on just how much you're up against, I recommend making a detailed list of the items using your emotional real estate. Later, you'll also be able to think strategically about how *you* want to rearrange it, because emotional real estate puts you back in the driver's seat.

In later chapters, I'll teach you how to take action on the things taking up emotional real estate, or simply let them go. You'll start slowly, with things you do every day, and by the end of this book, our goal is to bring emotional real estate to the same importance and clarity as time and money.

Taking conscious ownership in this way is incredibly empowering. No more looking out your window and wishing there weren't a burnt-out car sitting on the lawn. Upsetting things will still happen, but now you know you own that front yard—you have choices. You get to decide what stays or goes and what's planted, weeded, and watered.

Throughout the book, we'll include practices to use on your own or with a group. If you haven't set up a book club or guided study of this book, it's never too late. We're all learning to manage our emotional real estate together.

These are the first tools to use to manage your emotional real estate "property" and begin to create space for work-life wisdom. Think of them as the hammer and nails of your tool kit—the very simplest tools you can have. With them, you can build simple structures and fixtures that can improve your emotional real estate. Now, it's time to build your tool kit and create a life built on work-life wisdom. A life where there's room to be as busy as you want to be *and* as happy as you'd like.

EXERCISE #1: MAP YOUR EMOTIONAL REAL ESTATE

One of the first steps to mastering your emotional real estate is to gain awareness of what you are using that energy on each day.

- **Step 1:** Ask yourself, "What is using up my emotional real estate right now?" List everything on your emotional real estate on a piece of paper and get it out of your head as fast as you can. Just when you think you've got them all, ask yourself, "What else?" Flush them, like a detox. All the thoughts that swirl around your mind over and over again, the things you can't stop thinking about—get all of those down. Put on some headphones, close your eyes, do whatever you need to do in order to dump them on a piece of paper. You can draw or list or doodle—whatever you need to do to visualize the thoughts, worries, plans, emotions, and concerns filling your mind.

- **Step 2:** Next, score each item from one to ten based on how much emotional real estate each item is using up. How urgent or intense are they? How often are they coming up? Give a ten to the situations that keep you up at night, the anxieties that consume every waking moment. Assign a one to problems that cross your mind every once in a while, but don't seem like such a big deal. Other issues will fall somewhere in-between. Once you've listed all the thoughts using your emotional real estate and given each a score, take a step back and look at what stands out. What's glaring at you, and does it surprise you? Is it interesting that you scored one above the other? The numbers aren't necessarily prioritization as much as observation and assessment.

- **Step 3:** Now ask, "What are my biggest priorities right now? If I were to better manage my emotional real estate, how would I be allocating it today?" Notice if you see a gap anywhere!

One thing to note: Often, when I have people draw or list the things on their emotional real estate, they get mad that silly things are taking up so much space. It's not uncommon to respond with, "That's it! I'm *not* going to use up so much emotional real estate on my mother-in-law's Christmas dinner demands ever again!" Enjoy the observation and don't feel the need to do anything right now. In later chapters, we're going to work on letting things go or taking action. For now, just be curious and grow as much awareness as possible so we can dive into more work ahead.

CHAPTER FOUR

Climbing the State of Mind Ladder

Sometimes life knocks you on your ass. Get up. Get up. Get up. Happiness is not the absence of problems. It's the ability to deal with them.

—STEVE MARABOLI

Whenever you are about to act, ask yourself this question: "Is what I'm about to say or do going to bring me peace?" If the answer is yes, then go with it. If the answer is no, then remind yourself that it is your ego at work.

—WAYNE DYER

Now that we've gained an awareness around emotional real estate—there's another dimension to consider. You might have already noticed it. On a good day, it's easy to juggle all sorts of busyness, tasks, relationships, and whatever comes our way. But on a bad day, we might snap over the littlest things. Nothing new has been added on those days, but it *feels* different. That's because the state of mind we're in can affect the way we see and interact with our emotional real estate.

Imagine you're standing in your yard again, looking at the real estate available to you. From a spot at ground level, it can be hard to see beyond that big pile of junk in the middle of the lawn to the clearing on the other side— remember, beyond that pile is the present moment, and we want to access that as much as possible. It's hard to see that present space from ground level, but what if you had a ladder? You might climb up it and see that, actually, that pile of junk is not so large after all, and half the yard is completely empty. It's not as bad as you thought.

In this scenario, nothing about the situation in your yard has changed except your view of it. Standing on the top rungs of the ladder, you're occupying a more expansive space. From way up there, you can gather a holistic view and still enjoy the sight of the present moment beyond your front yard.

In a high state of mind, we feel empowered, creative, and proactive. We have plenty of resources available to think clearly and purposefully. In a higher state of mind, broader thinking and a bigger vision begin to bubble up.

Our best ideas, best solutions, and best performance exist in this state of mind.

At other times, when we've booked every last minute of the day and still have too many deadlines and not enough time, on top of responding to the nasty emails sitting in our inbox, the weight of it all will pull us down the ladder. Hanging out on the very lowest rung, feelings like anger, frustration, irritation, resentfulness, and defensiveness can take over. It may even feel like it's not worth even trying to clear out your emotional real estate. *It's too hard, so why bother?*

When you spend too much time in a low state of mind, burnout kicks in. There's not even enough energy to be angry or disappointed anymore—we simply move to apathy. That's the lowest state of mind there is. Since there's no room left for frustration, you just have to check out.

And as transformative coaching methods teach, our minds are always in flux. A person's perception of the world is not static; what we observe and how we behave depends largely on how we feel and think at the moment— the ladder on the lawn, or state of mind. Just as important as identifying what's filling up our emotional real estate, we have to learn to identify where we are on the state of mind ladder and how that's affecting the way we see and process our circumstances.

LET'S GET INTO THE LADDER BUSINESS

The best example of state of mind in action was explained to me by a coach and former therapist named George Pransky. In one of his lectures, he was talking about how, when he used to practice relationship counseling, he'd bring a frustrated and fighting couple into a room together and start by having them talk about the problems they were facing. Oftentimes, within ten minutes, one was in tears while the other was angry and shutting down, and then he would attempt to get them to engage in a conversation around how to improve their relationship. Later in his career, he began to understand how state of mind directly influences one's ability to creatively problem solve. He'd now invite a similar exhausted couple into his office and begin the conversation with a discussion around why these two people felt committed to protecting and growing the love they have for one another. As both parties would begin to speak and start to creep into a higher state of mind, each person's ability to problem solve expanded, along with the open-mindedness needed to see the same situation through a brand new lens.

In a similar example, I learned about state of mind when I started my business. I had done so much visualization work through NLP that putting in my notice meant it was definitely happening. Unfortunately, this was in 2008. Specifically, I left my job on October 1, and Lehman

Brothers had filed for bankruptcy on September 22. The economy literally crashed two weeks before my last day.

I was terrified, and my state of mind was a wreck. My thoughts were constantly spiraling around the negative: *Oh my God. Why did this happen to me? Why did I do this now? I have no money in the bank! What made me think I could do this? How could I think I was smart enough to start a successful business?*

In this low state of mind, the obstacles in front of me seemed insurmountable, and well-meaning people kept coming up to me with tempting suggestions. They'd ask if I'd thought about selling technology or taking a part-time job here or trying this opportunity there. And I was so full of fear about my ability to make my own dreams come true that I almost jumped on their offers. I was so close to giving up and putting energy into other people's dreams. *Maybe I did need to scrap my business and go work on somebody else's.*

That's when I sat down with Bob Miller—the founder of Miller Heiman—who was around eighty years old at the time. He was famous for spouting wisdom to anyone who would listen, given he had acquired so much of it in his lifetime. When I asked him his opinion about the failing economy, he was incredibly calm and collected about it. Throughout his career, he had seen the economy go up and down so many times that the current crisis seemed little more than another bump in the road. He didn't think the sky was falling. He told me, "The economy will just serve as another excuse people will use to avoid making things happen. Right now is when the real opportunities are there."

His perspective from the top of the ladder allowed him to see this as a blip on the radar. I, being in a low state of mind, was mad at the circumstances and wanted him to feel bad for me too—I wanted him to empathize with my situation. Instead, his state of mind was optimistic and empowered.

He said, "The best of the best are the people who see the rise and fall in the economy but don't use it to explain their results; they know it's their attitude, capability, and actions that generate results."

He left no room for excuses. His question was simply, "How are you going to make this successful, given the opportunities that exist right now in this economy?"

His state of mind was a tool for him and not a trap. Our goal for this chapter is to ask ourselves: given our circumstances and state of mind, what are we going to *do* next?

WHAT INFLUENCES YOUR STATE OF MIND?

Steve Chandler, my former coach, taught me about state of mind and the distinction between owner mentality and victim mentality. He taught me that in a high state of mind, we're using owner mentality, which is incredibly empowered. When we feel like an owner, we know we can make things happen and get things done. We're focused on what we're trying to create. Owner mentality moves us forward in a positive way while still letting us focus on the present in a mindful way.

Victim mentality, on the other hand, is unempowered. Sometimes it's blame-focused. This is "Why me?" thinking. Thinking like a victim can seem like the easy way out, because it absolves us of responsibility—or we can be so accountable that we start to kick dirt in our own faces. After all, this terrible thing has happened to you and there's nothing you can do about it, right? Unfortunately, the victim mindset also seriously disempowers us and limits our possibilities. I could have easily stayed in this mentality in 2008. *Of course it would happen to me. I would be the one to open a business five minutes after the economy fell into the abyss.*

You can take an inventory of what's filling up your emotional real estate at any time, but it's important to realize that your perspective of those things will shift over time. Sometimes your next steps seem clear and manageable—

your insights will guide you to let go of some things taking up too much space, and give you energy to heave the deadfall into the dumpster. Other times, the chaos that stands in your way overwhelms you, and it's all you can do to clear a narrow path so you can trudge from one end to the other.

Where you stand on the state of mind ladder at a given moment directly influences the quality of your thinking. When you're happily perched on the highest rungs, you feel peaceful, motivated, and engaged. You may feel optimistic, even euphoric. But when you walk into a meeting after watching a depressing news story, you may interpret every word your colleagues say as negative or discouraging.

When I first started my business, my routine was to get up in the morning, have my cup of coffee and enjoy the great mood that comes with it, then sit down to watch the news. Every single time, my state of mind would drop six rungs. Disasters of all kinds filled my mind and activated all those negative, fear-based thoughts. *The economy is failing. I might never get a job again. I might never have enough money. The bank might foreclose on my house. My retirement might be gone. And did you hear about that tragedy and those poor people? Did you hear about that crime—how could someone do that? And by the way, it's actually going to rain again?!* And on and on. Every morning, I'd fuel those negative thoughts. And every morning, I'd crash to the bottom of my ladder.

All the problems in my emotional real estate would feel even more insurmountable thanks to all that energy I'd spent thinking about those terrible what-ifs. Simply turning on the television in the morning was impacting my state of mind so much that I struggled to find the resources for the one thing that should have been taking up most of my emotional real estate: thinking creatively and taking action to get my business off the ground. I'd take in all these messages about the worst economy ever, then sit at my desk wondering, "I don't think I can do this." Victim mentality would kick in, and I would procrastinate taking action and decide to clean my office one more time.

One afternoon I was listening to some podcasts on positive thinking, and I had an epiphany: I needed to change my routine. So, I decided on a detox from morning news and instead, in the morning, I would turn to Hay House Radio, a podcast channel featuring positive inspirational speakers. I decided that I was going to start my day with filtered information, with ideas that came from positive psychology and not attention-grabbing headlines. I figured if something really important happened, my mom would call me.

When I stopped filling my head with doom and gloom

"the sky is falling" messages first thing every day and replaced them with some "I can do it!" thoughts each day, I found I had a lot more energy to take action throughout the morning. Instead of crashing, I still had plenty of that first-coffee energy by ten or eleven, and I felt good about the work I had to do for the day.

You may have already noticed that both the ability to evaluate your emotional real estate and to assess your state of mind are tools that you can use to make a difference in your life right now. In a similar way, owner and victim mindsets aren't static, and you need to observe your fluctuating mentality before you can shift it. If moving up and down a ladder isn't quite the visual you need, picture mentality as a radio station frequency that you can tune into. As you turn the dial, you can listen to what's coming out of the speakers. Listen carefully, because what you hear will reflect your state of mind.

Start by paying attention to your quality of thinking in different states of mind. When you're frustrated or upset, do you fall into a victim mentality, thinking the world has done you wrong and there's nothing to be done? When you're feeling curious and creative, do you see yourself as more of an owner? Most often, a victim mindset will follow a low state of mind, and an owner mindset will rise from a high state of mind.

EXERCISE #2: SPOT OWNER MENTALITY AND STOP VICTIM MENTALITY

It's critical to grow awareness to when a thought is coming from victim mentality or owner mentality. It's easy to shift mindset when you can easily see where your thoughts are coming from.

- **Step 1:** When do you hear yourself thinking victim mentality thoughts? List as many examples as you can think of. (Hint: we all do this sometimes!)

Examples:

- I just don't have enough time. I can't get this done. It's her fault this is such a mess. If he wasn't so mean, we could be happier.

- There's nothing I can do—guess I just have to put up with it. Nothing is going to change unless he/she/they change.

- **Step 2:** Where could you transition that victim mentality thought into an owner mentality thought?

Instead of focusing on the issue or what feels broken, try asking yourself, "What am I trying to create?" or "What would I like to see in the future?" or "What can I do to influence this situation?" Move your attention and focus from what is fixed, to where you have influence. Finding where you are empowered in any situation helps you move up the state of mind ladder and really reduces the amount of space you feel something is taking up in your emotional real estate.

LIFE HAPPENS ALL OVER THE LADDER

If we were to plot these concepts on a piece of graph paper, emotional real estate would exist on a horizontal x-axis, and state of mind would work vertically, on a y-axis. It's the ladder overlooking the lawn. As state of mind moves up and down the state of mind axis, we naturally see our emotional real estate from a variety of perspectives.

It's tempting to seek a way to stay on the highest rung of the state of mind ladder all the time and just banish those low thoughts forever—but constant, over-the-moon euphoria doesn't lead to the best decisions either. Besides, it's not realistic to think we can be bubbling with happiness each moment. Some of the most brilliant, optimistic, happy people still have moments or days where they drop into a low state of mind. Like learning to allow thoughts to come and go as we meditate, we can appreciate that state of mind will always shift just by virtue of being human.

The key is to grow awareness around what state of mind we are in. When you begin to observe your own patterns more as part of an awareness of emotional real estate and state of mind, you'll notice that 99 percent of the time, a low mood eventually lifts. State of mind will always change, guaranteed. Once you accept that state of mind is constantly shifting, you can harness that knowledge by using different states for different tasks. The question shifts from, "How do I become and stay happy all the time?" to, "How do I leverage state of mind as it fluctuates?" Not only can you give yourself permission to have those low thoughts and let them pass, but you can plan to use low and high states of mind more efficiently throughout your day.

When you better understand your own patterns, you can choose the right times to make decisions or deal with situations that will give you the best possible outcome. When you realize a fluctuating state of mind is simply part of your internal makeup—and acknowledge that you won't be approaching situations from the same perspective every time—you can begin to recognize how it impacts the outcome each time. This awareness allows you to come up with transformative ways of thinking about things.

In fact, you might already have some insight into your changing state of mind. You may realize how it changes over the course of a year as events, goals, and activities shift with the seasons. If your business is busy in the fall, you might recognize overwhelm starting to set in as demand picks up. When the pace slows down again in January, you probably find it easier to get into a creative thinking mindset again. Or you might start to notice that you feel low on the Thursday morning after a parent-teacher conference, because you're still processing what happened at the meeting the night before. You might find that after the monthly board meeting, you are frustrated, tired, and your state of mind is low.

Notice when your willpower and resilience feel highest. If you know you're naturally in an expansive mood in the mornings, that's probably a great time to tackle a challenge, solve a problem, or deal with that nasty email you've been avoiding. On the other hand, when you're exhausted at eight o'clock at night, it's probably *not* a great time to try to get ahead by tackling those emails. Or maybe you realize that you're a night person who gets your second wind at three in the afternoon and can make better decisions then. Recognizing these natural energy levels throughout the course of the day or a season can help you identify your state of mind on a more granular level.

MIRRORING STATES OF MIND

Once you learn to manage your internal awareness of your own state of mind, you can become conscious of what other people might be experiencing in their state of mind. If I have a coaching client who's completely overwhelmed and frustrated, and I'm supposed to be coaching them on something complex and life-changing, I want to give them some space first. It's not a great time for them to put their problem-solver hat on. In fact, if you want to create regret, make decisions in a low state of mind.

A director I was working with called me to say his company had conducted an employee engagement survey and he'd just gotten back his results. "They were terrible," he said. "Nobody's happy. Everybody on my team is miserable." Without pausing, he continued with his solution: "So I pulled my three managers into a room and told them they had to fix it, or someone's getting fired."

The director immediately dropped to a low state of mind when he got those results, then demanded creative thinking about a complex problem from team members who were suddenly worried about being fired. Their state of mind began to mirror his, and they had nothing for him. In his low state of mind, the director had dragged his team down as well. Then, after he pulled everyone else down low, he expected creative thinking and results that are much more challenging to produce in a lower state of mind.

On the other hand, I was recently working with a vice president and her director. I don't know what specifically was going on, but before we began our discussion, the vice president checked in with her director as she knew he had been dealing with a challenge that morning.

She said, "Is now a good time for you to tackle this?" When he said yes, she said, "Are you sure? This can wait if you don't feel fully present for this discussion." Obviously, she knew he was struggling and likely in a low state of mind. She was checking in with him to see if he had the emotional real estate available to take that Monday morning call or not.

We can become aware of this dynamic in our close relationships, as well. Maybe your spouse made a nasty comment you took personally. When you notice that they're dealing with something that put them in a low state of mind, you can recognize they're probably not doing their best thinking at the moment, which might soften the way you hear and process the comment.

MIND THE GAP

Surprise! If you are like me, some surprises are good news, but on most days, I'm trying to avoid surprises. A wise person once told me that the gap between what we expect and what actually happens directly relates to how we feel and experience that situation. If we are expecting traffic during rush hour on a Friday night, although we may not enjoy it, we still seem to inch our way through. But that same thirty-minute delay on a normally slow traffic day can drive us crazy. The difference between what we expect and what happens can change our position on the state of mind ladder by several rungs.

So, when we get hit with one of those "unpleasant" surprises and people feel angry and upset, our first instinct is to react; everyone wants to know what to *do next*. So, it's ironic that when I'm coaching a client in this situation, I often strategize with them on how they can do *nothing*. Sometimes, the best way to bridge that gap, or respond to disappointment, is to allow time for your state of mind to improve on its own. One thing we know for sure is that all of us have a fluctuating state of mind. And if we know that, we know a low state of mind is not permanent. So just hitting pause in a low state of mind is one of the easiest ways to strategize how to respond when life hands you a lemon...in the face.

During the 2016 US presidential election, I was excited about the potential that election held. When election night came around, I cracked open a beautiful bottle of wine to watch the vote counts roll in, expecting to be celebrating with millions of other people (especially so many women who were excited to see a historical first take place). Of course, things took a very different turn. That was *not* how I thought I would spend that bottle of wine. That was not the plan. What was supposed to be a victory toast wound up a weak consolation.

The next day, I was asked to write a blog for a magazine offering my opinion on the election and perspective on the winner. This blog would be reaching a significant audience.

I was in such a low state of mind that my thoughts on the topic didn't feel constructive. I didn't feel good about what I could put together for the world to see—I didn't feel like I could gather up an intelligent response.

But I was aware of my state of mind and how it might affect my work, so I asked for a small extension on the deadline, and I managed to give myself space to see if I'd feel a bit better after having time to absorb this information. Although there was a huge gap between what I'd anticipated would happen and what had actually transpired, I needed to access a higher state of mind to find some creativity. In other words, I simply recognized my state of mind, then paused to give it time to shift a little bit.

After a lot of processing, I'll admit I was still disappointed, but I was getting more clarity. To center my thoughts a bit, I had to think outside the box. I sat in the quiet space of my office and asked myself, *If I were in a higher state of mind, what perspective might I bring to the topic?* I spent some time reflecting on this question, and that small shift moved me into more productive thinking. The piece I wound up writing was more insightful than anything I could have brought to the table that first day.

Some of the biggest consumers of emotional real estate are events that we expected to happen that didn't, or outcomes we didn't expect at all. So, should we lower our expectations? Lose them altogether? Absolutely not.

If you expect your marriage to be "until death do you part," receiving divorce papers would absolutely rock your world. That doesn't mean you should discard those expectations and live life expecting your partner to leave you at any moment. That's not any healthier. If the unwanted outcome does arrive, though, you have the choice to be aware that the magnitude of your emotional upheaval is directly related to the beliefs and expectations you have held onto for so long. What you planned was so far from how things turned out, no wonder you're upset!

There is deep wisdom in being able to say, "I'm feeling frustrated because I didn't expect this to happen." Recognize the emotion as you're going through the experience and you'll notice something fascinating—merely acknowledging the difference between what you thought would happen and what did happen takes a lot of the negative energy out of the moment.

WAIT FOR THE SUNSHINE

Waiting a while can be just what we need to do to gain clarity, even for the biggest concerns of life. A client of mine, Bev, called me in the middle of February, on a cold, blizzardy day. She was very frustrated with her marriage and decided she couldn't take it anymore and wanted a divorce. She and her husband had a child together, and between their family life and stressful jobs, they often found themselves in the middle of nasty fights each week. When I started to inquire more about what was on her emotional real estate, I could tell she still loved him and there was no abuse or cheating—but she had an enormous number of things weighing on her, including chasing doctors to help her daughter with a medical condition, an aging parent who needed a lot of help, and a job she didn't feel very valued at. When I asked about her husband's emotional real estate, she paused—she hadn't thought much about his. Upon second thought, he had a lot, too—some similar things and some different.

What I especially noticed as she spoke was her low state of mind—her frustration, her anger, how depressed she seemed. I challenged her to consider if the problems she was upset about were temporary or permanent.

"If you want to get divorced," I suggested, "wait until June. If the relationship is so bad that you need a divorce, it will still be worth ending in June."

I encouraged her to acknowledge that, with both of them running low on available emotional real estate while suffering through a particularly cold and dark winter, it was possible that things might change with time, without her having to change him. With a little bit of time, vitamin D, and a higher state of mind, she might get more clarity on whether leaving her marriage was the right decision. We spent the rest of the session working on a few other things currently on her emotional real estate.

When I met with her again in June, she felt a bit sheepish. She was still married, and things were a lot better. Ironically enough, she said when May and June rolled around and they were each enjoying more sun (i.e. shoveling less snow), the problems just didn't feel that big anymore. They both relaxed a bit about things that had once provoked big fights. Some fun summer plans to look forward to, along with the tincture of time, helped her decisions to become clearer. We had a great conversation about how differently problems can look when you are in a higher state of mind.

So often, we can find ourselves saying, "The sky is falling!" at the exact time we need inspired, original thinking that's free from panic. An anxious, low state of mind can block access to the clear thinking we need. That doesn't mean it's wrong to feel upset or angry. It's okay to not know how to get back up again right now. All we really need is the self-awareness to realize that the bad feeling in the situation isn't permanent.

In a response to a crisis, make a game plan to figure out how to do as little as possible in terms of heavy decision-making and complex problem-solving for a brief period of time. Slow things down for a few minutes, hours, or days, depending on the situation. Make the space to gain perspective, process what's happening, and come back to it from a higher state of mind. Give it a little bit of time until you have more optimistic thoughts again and can make it back to a high state of mind.

My coaching clients confess that waiting it out is harder than it seems. People often act based on their immediate emotional response—they're quick to quit their job, sell their house, end their relationship, fire an employee, put their child in boarding school, whatever the case may be. "I just didn't have the strength to change my state of mind before sending that email," they'd tell me. "I just had to respond." Making a big decision looks like the only way to find relief.

Remember: this is not about strength; it's about time.

Big decisions might happen at a low state of mind, but the *best* decisions happen at a higher level. If you get bad news in a meeting and you feel like crying or punching the wall when it's over, realize you'll probably feel differently tomorrow morning. You'll wake up with access to different information, clarity, and ideas, and you'll be in a different state of mind. In the heat of the moment, processing what's happening seems impossible, but taking time to process is one way of moving up the ladder and levering a higher state of mind to come to a more creative approach.

State of mind can help or hinder everything we do; it

shapes the type of creativity, discernment, and clarity we're able to bring to a challenge. Instead of getting caught under the incredible weight of a low state of mind and seeing only one way out, we'll start to see more options.

PERMISSION TO BE LOW

The problems we are facing are human conditions. The goal is not to escape the things that bring us down or to create a life in which we are never down. We're shooting for resilience here. We want to be able to get up—to overcome the things that are inevitably going to get in our way when we're solving problems or managing conflict or making decisions.

Understanding the power of state of mind doesn't mean adopting a Pollyanna attitude. I'm not asking you to walk around every day singing show tunes. When you begin to understand state of mind, though, it is like accessing a little bit of magic. You'll begin to see your relationships with other people differently. You'll be able to acknowledge the role that their state of mind plays when you ask them to solve problems or think about things.

Sometimes, we just have to make peace with our low state of mind, while acknowledging that a better perspective will come. Telling yourself that you must snap out of a low state can leave you without the permission to just feel what's real. It's also okay to hold a negative emotion for a while. Own it. Keep it. Giving yourself permission to feel what you feel is healthy; it's not the same as wallowing in your misery.

We especially need to give ourselves permission to be disappointed. Too often, the self-help world allows us only a short time to feel down before we're expected to come

---

THE RAINY DAY FILE

When I started my business, one of my coaches gave me this trick: *take every positive note that a client sent to tell me that I added value to his or her life and put it in a testimonials file.* He told me to save that file for a rainy day, for the days when I would feel like I hadn't added value to anyone's life. That file should be ready, right at my fingertips, so that I could see someone saying, "Thank you. That helped."

Those times did come, just like he told me they would. Maybe a project didn't go well, or a coaching call didn't go well. Even just knowing that the folder was there—all those responses from people who've gotten value from things that I've helped them with—can turn around my mood.

Recently I was coaching a client who took this concept and made it his own. He decided to create a collection of pictures that were from the most wonderful moments of his life. He labeled the file "What matters most." Again, when feeling low, he knew that if he took just ten minutes to scan those shots of his favorite vacations, moments he felt madly in love, moments belly laughing with friends, and moments adoring his family and beloved pets, it would help him access his high state of mind by helping him remember what matters most.

---

up with a way to be happy again. When I started coaching, I was using a lot of tools from NLP, so I was always looking to quickly reframe negative experiences as positive. At the same time, I found I couldn't do it myself. It was impossible for me to just reframe a negative experience and feel better five minutes later. For both myself and my clients, I had to find peace in the moments themselves.

It's counterintuitive, but sitting with the bad feelings often allows the healing to come faster. It took over ten years of education for me to understand this: the minute we give ourselves permission to feel crappy, the internal battle is over. It's a relief.

While you're holding that low feeling, be curious about it. Ask yourself questions. After deciding to do nothing, think about what you can ask yourself in order to reach that higher level. *If I were in a higher state of mind, what new perspective might I bring to this topic I'm contemplating?* Maybe you're still rolled up on the floor in a ball, but now you can see—and maybe reach—the first rungs of the ladder that will eventually pull you up.

Remember that a fluctuating state of mind isn't a state of being or something that you're stuck with. You can influence, and even change, your state of mind. A ladder is just another tool, and we're going to use these tools to clear and maintain our emotional real estate. If you become aware that you're in a slump, you can make a conscious decision to think through ways to create movement out of that lousy spot. Maybe you just need to get up, get out of the office, and grab a coffee. Or maybe picking up a positive book or watching a funny clip might help you shift.

When you pause to think through these steps regularly, you'll start to notice what triggers you to fall into that low state—what circumstances lead you to take inappropriate actions based on your dim view of the world.

Often, for example, certain people—such as coworkers or family members—predictably shift your state of mind. If you know you have to deal with that person, how can you change your state of mind to create a better outcome? Is there a better or worse time to approach them? If you've had a bad night's sleep and woke up in a terrible mood, it might not be the best time to march up to your coworker's desk and tell them what you really think about that email last night.

Pay attention to when you choose to deal with difficult situations. Keep in mind that your best performance and decisions come from neutral or a high state of mind in those moments.

EXERCISE #3: MAP YOUR STATE OF MIND

It's critical to be able to visualize what state of mind looks like and quickly realize how it's influencing you in each situation.

- **Step 1:** Ask yourself: "When was the last time I felt like I was in a high state of mind? What circumstances put me there?" When you're in a high state of mind, what's going on? What's happening with your emotional real estate? How does this help you learn something?

- **Step 2:** What are some moments you can think of in which you were in a low state of mind? What was the quality of your thinking in those moments? What were some of the thoughts you had when you were in that low state of mind?

- **Step 3:** Reaching for the empowering belief is one of the faster ways to shift state of mind. If I wanted to change my state of mind using an empowering belief, what empowering belief would I need to focus on in this situation?" (Example: I am strong. I am smart. I have the tools I need to do amazing in this situation. I know I will feel differently about this situation in a higher state of mind, etc.)

Part Three

Bringing
Concepts into
Practice

CHAPTER FIVE

Property Management 101

*The smallest of implementations is always worth more than
the grandest of intentions.*

—ROBIN SHARMA

*You'll never change your life until you change something
you do daily. The secret of your success is found in your
daily routine.*

—JOHN C. MAXWELL

Awareness of emotional real estate and state of mind is,
in itself, a giant step forward. You know how to check in
with your state of mind at a given moment and make decisions differently as a result. You know that when you're
wasting energy on something low priority it may be a poor
use of your emotional real estate. Once you can visualize

the concept of emotional real estate and state of mind in this way, you can't ever "un-see" it. It's an awareness you see in every moment you perceived as stress—you have insights around how to get a clearer view of what is really happening behind the scenes.

But now what? What do we do with all that great awareness?

When we finally look out on our life's front lawn and realize it's overcrowded and a mess, it's easy to want to shut the blinds and never look outside again. While there are some people who can go live on a mountain somewhere and find complete simplicity, peace, and happiness, that's not the only option we have. It's okay to have ambitions, interests, and priorities that we want to include in our lives—to be busy *and* happy.

The number one mission, then—the goal of all this work and the one thing you should take away if you don't even read another page of this book—is to consistently operate with some amount of free space on your emotional real estate. Free space is how you can become present. Free space is how you can stay busy without losing yourself or your happiness. Free space is what gives you room to process the unexpected without feeling overwhelmed.

With that said, in any given moment, we have one of two options in front of us in order to create that free space:

we can let something go, or we can take action. That's Property Management 101, and it's how we can bring happiness and presence back into our lives.

HOW TO (CONSISTENTLY) OPERATE WITH FREE SPACE

There's a math to emotional real estate—and not the frustrating math your kids come home with or the high-level math you either loved or hated in college. If you have a really good picture of your emotional real estate as a bulky front lawn, all of the baggage, fixtures, junk, and landscaping stand between you and the presence that sits on the other side of that lawn. In our case, the "beyond" is the present moment. The only way to have access to that present moment—to being happy no matter how busy you are—is to keep some free space. Always. With enough room for all the busyness you've planned and intentionally included, as well as a cushion for the inevitable surprises of life.

The way to make that happen is with the math of emotional real estate: we can either subtract things that use up unnecessary real estate or add things that give back energy or space. That's really it. We are going to start with things that take up space, and for those things, we have three options: we can consciously choose to use emotional real estate on something, choose to let it go, or take action on it.

Before we just add a life-changing meditation or yoga practice to our plate, I want to mention that when I work with clients who feel overwhelmed, the last thing they want to hear is that they need to "find time" for something else in order to feel happy. They are running at full capacity all the time and simply feel helpless to prioritize their energy. If you are like me, you've already heard it all—through books, speakers, and advice that says, "Do these things to feel less stress"—get in exercise, eat right for more energy, find time to meditate, hit a local yoga class...all the while, this is one more obligation to add to your day and potentially fail to deliver on. When I read all of those books about being happy, none of them taught me *how* to be happy—they only told me that I *should* be happy. Similarly, when my clients come to me, they aren't ready to add another practice.

Untangling the things that fill up our emotional real estate can feel like being caught in a tornado, though realistically, we aren't in any danger. My clients come into coaching calls often feeling like life is so busy it's about to crash into a wall but meanwhile, when you get outside of their head, their house is still standing, their car is still safely parked in the driveway, the dog is still wagging his tail, and their partner and kids are (mostly) happy and healthy. Yet their world *feels* like busy, unmanageable chaos. It can seem impossible to give enough energy and thought to all the things they are being pulled and called to do. They are lacking basic property management skills—the math of emotional real estate.

EMOTIONAL REAL ESTATE IN ANY ASPECT OF LIFE

The awareness you've developed and the tools you're going to learn around emotional real estate can really apply to your whole life. It's for the issues you face at work, the relationship you have with your boss, life with your significant other, and historic issues with your parents, just as much as it is for your cluttered basement or the porch you need to rebuild or the chores your teenager won't do. It's for the stuff that comes up randomly throughout the day and for family baggage you're dealing with from years ago.

In this chapter, we're going to start to make space for those bigger, long-term changes by getting big returns on small shifts now. As long as we keep emotional real estate front and center, starting small is a great way to create a little bit of breathing room that allows us to think more clearly about everything else. So, picture yourself putting all those other issues into boxes and setting them on the edge of your front lawn. We're going to get to them. But first, we're going to get some practice in.

START SMALL (REALLY SMALL)

A full emotional real estate feels messy and difficult to unravel, especially when the day to day seems too pressing. Often, this is where we think being "too busy" comes from—we blame the impending deadlines and full schedules for our frustration. We might even rearrange and reorganize our schedules, trying to create some space on the calendar. The problem is, every time we rearrange the planner and map out deadlines and try to "fix" our daily routines, we rarely have emotional real estate in mind while we do it. Perceived stress is occurring as a result of mindset and self-talk, which includes past concerns and future worries and everything that we're going to unravel in the rest of the book.

With as much as I've worked on emotional real estate over the years, I've never been able to fully compartmentalize different ways to deal with different aspects of emotional real estate, because *everything* that is happening in our minds takes up emotional real estate. And since we feel our thinking, we are talking about the entire experience of life. The good news is, you really can apply this one framework and set of tools to every aspect of your life, big or small, in whatever way you need in order to create space.

What I have found, however, is that the things that take up space on emotional real estate are happening in one of three spaces: they are in the past, are currently facing us in the present, or are a concern for the future. Or, you can split it down into two buckets: thoughts that take up space, or activity that takes up energy.

So, if we need more emotional real estate to be happy, then our basic options are to let go or take action on a thought. Since it's pretty difficult to think of a way to take action on a thing that happened in the past, oftentimes, letting go becomes critical.

If you're still losing sleep over your sister's remark that she made two years ago about how you didn't know how to do Thanksgiving dinner correctly, it's taking up far too much space, and you'll have to let it go in order to create that space. More on that in chapter six.

Or, you might be thinking a lot about the future, planning and strategizing and even worrying or feeling fear. When that happens, there might be some expectations you need to let go, or you might be able to put a plan of action in place that makes you feel more empowered about the steps in front of you. More on taking action in chapter seven.

In the present, there's often a mix of options available for us to let some things go and take action on other things. We'll work on daily life first, practicing emotional real estate management with the small things before we tackle the more pressing concerns and prominent challenges, in later chapters. Our goal with emotional real estate is not to prescribe a canned "do this" list but more to help you find a practice that is customized just for *you* and *your* busy life.

A CLOSER LOOK AT YOUR DAY

Managing emotional real estate is not unlike managing a schedule or a budget. Oftentimes when I'm working with clients, I ask them to walk me through their typical day. I ask for blow-by-blow detail. There are normally some very easy ways to find new emotional real estate if we look closely.

In fact, as we've discussed a bit already, they can be intertwined. For example, we might consider our budgets when we wonder whether we can afford to spend $100 to hire a cleaner, thinking how much we'd hate to spend that finite amount of money on something we could rearrange and do in a few hours ourselves. That said, if we think of how much emotional real estate someone might use each day looking at the dirty bathroom floors thinking, "I've got to find time to clean the house. My God, please don't let a friend drop by unexpected" or, "Geez, my life feels like a mess" (while staring at a literal mess), the cost benefit of spending that $100 could give back what feels like $300 of emotional real estate.

Another example includes reading or watching the news reports over your morning coffee each day. If you start to notice that you head into your day thinking about serial murders and the latest war that's brewing, you may want to re-think this step in your day to better optimize your emotional real estate. I'm not saying bury your head in the sand—but figure out how to stay informed while understanding what some of these stories can do to your emotional real estate. If you are just scrolling, reading, or listening to bad news out of habit, how do you feel afterward? When you shut off the news, do you feel your head spinning as you replay the stories of the day?

Once, my client decided to pick two new topics that she wanted to stay informed on daily because they were the ones she cared most about. She's decided to actively get involved with two organizations as a result. She now reads a weekly news blog summary so she's in the know on world events.

When I teach sessions on this, the process of re-thinking the day through the lens of emotional real estate is usually full of aha moments for people when they start to really look closely. One day I was teaching a workshop and a participant named Stella told me about how there was one coworker she had who always sent evening emails, and those emails would always piss her off. She'd find herself going to bed mad about the comments, unable to sleep, thinking about her response, and brewing in frustration.

The obvious solution is: why don't you stop checking emails at night and stay present with your family? "I don't have that kind of job," she told me. "We work with other parts of the country, and there's an expectation that we'll be available outside of our own business hours."

Her aha moment came later. In my next session with her, she announced that she had found a solution. "I realized how important it was, so I got creative last night after our session."

Stella went back that evening and changed the settings on her inbox, so that every email from that coworker that came in was automatically filtered to a different folder. She loved this solution because she didn't have to see those unread emails waiting for her at night. In the morning, when Stella got to the office, she could open that folder and start working on those tasks in a higher state of mind. She was much more patient in her responses, and she was finally able to sleep at night.

Stella's solution was utterly simple but absolutely brilliant. It fit her situation perfectly. She knew that the emails from her colleague were coming at the wrong time of day. That one simple shift in how she organized her day and the way she interacted with a task that was draining and frustrating changed everything from the quality of her interaction with this person to the quality of her performance to the quality of her sleep.

Small changes, just like this, can make a big impact.

UNDERSTAND YOUR INSTINCTS

It should go without saying that there are parts of your day that you just don't enjoy. It's true for all of us. But let's not take that for granted—most of us come into this work with some unpacking to do. Remember that most of the stress and extra busyness we're perceiving is a result of the thoughts we are experiencing. Often, if you think about your thought patterns throughout the day, you probably don't have a clear mindset about the parts of your day that align with your instincts and the those that don't. Instead, you're probably doing what I did, and what many of my clients have done: you beat yourself up.

God, why don't I like this?

Why am I procrastinating again—can't I just suck it up and get it done?

I can easily do this [insert work, activity, hobby], but for some reason, I feel drained afterwards.

I just need to work harder or toughen up a bit—stop whining!

Years after I left my first job in engineering, I was working with a consultant who told me she had this "amazing tool" for understanding whether people were a good fit for certain jobs at work. It was an assessment tool online, and after I took it, she and I talked about the results.

She pointed out how I came back with high improvisation instincts—that I'm an ideas person, scoring nine out of ten. But my data analysis and repeatable process instincts were closer to a four. We laughed, and I had some aha moments, but then she told me this:

> "I can't believe you were ever an engineer. I'm not surprised you were capable of doing the job, but none of your instincts actually align with what you'd need to enjoy that job. No wonder you used to beat yourself because you weren't happy at work."

Her point then, and what I've seen play out over and over since, is not that we *can't* do many different types of work, but that different people have different instincts—things that they'd love to do just for fun. And even though we *aren't* left to our own devices, we all get energized by different types of work based on our instincts. One person might do something very repetitively or detail- and process-oriented, while another person (ahem, like *me*) would want to get creative and think outside the box. Some of us want the instructions, while others don't want the answers—we want to figure it out in our own way.

Back before I understood how instincts work, I honestly wondered if there was something wrong with me—for some reason, my highly repetitive, Excel-sheet-driven job as an engineer was so draining to me. Understanding how instinct influences emotional real estate helps us understand that some things are an energy suck and others are not, and that it's different for everyone. And that's absolutely okay.

This doesn't mean we have to or even *can* avoid tasks that don't align with who we are. Most of us spend the whole day running into things that don't match our instincts. You may love to travel, but that comes with expense reports that you still have to do. You might outsource your taxes and finances to an accountant, but you still need to make sure you are organized to have the information on hand in tax season (uh, does anyone actually *love* organizing a year's worth of receipts in one sitting?).

There will always be things that are tiring that we don't necessarily enjoy. When we identify what those tasks are, we can stop beating ourselves up for not enjoying them!

Begin to plan your day so that you can approach those

tasks from a higher state of mind. Gain some energy and free space from tasks you're inclined to enjoy and use that space to get through the things you don't. Start re-thinking how you plan your energy for those tasks.

GAMEDAY DECISIONS

We've circled all the way back around to the question we started the chapter with: what do we do with all that awareness? If we're seeing the things that drain energy or give back, what does that actually mean for our day-to-day lives? Like Stella did when she realized how much emotional real estate she was losing to such a small thing, it's time for us to look at our lives through the lens of emotional real estate and start to get creative.

Again, start simple—really simple. You might be surprised by how much emotional real estate you can free up by going on a mental diet, clearing out the noise that comes from social media, news, email, and television.

One client told me how angry she gets every time she's on Facebook. *These crazy people! What are they thinking?!* So, I challenged her to a Facebook fast, and she took me up on it. A couple of weeks after deleting the app from her phone, she couldn't believe how much better she felt. When she went back on Facebook six or eight months later, she was ready. She hid people and topics she didn't want to use emotional real estate on, she was more mindful about what she shared, and she stopped engaging in conversations that didn't serve her.

The next step is to begin to rearrange. Notice which of your activities bring your state of mind down and which push it higher. Stella had to respond to those emails no matter what, but when she did it in the morning, she was able to handle it much more efficiently for everyone involved. If a great morning puts you in a high state of mind, knock out that frustrating task right after it while you're still riding that high.

Finally, let's let go of the things that we don't actually have to do every day. Can you take on more of the work that you love and delegate some of the work that uses up a lot of emotional real estate? If you dread meal planning, can you outsource it? Or, could you eat the same meals each week or each month to reduce the required emotional real estate around it? Can you hire someone to do some of the tasks around the house that use up a lot of space? Or, if you love Saturday morning cleaning time and it charges you up, enjoy it! Make space for that every weekend—plan to turn on some music and decompress.

Getting into the practice of optimizing the day around our energy levels and instincts can also help us to pivot when the unexpected hits. I remember working with a client whose laptop melted down on the day of an important presentation. Her executive vice president had been calling her, she was waiting for IT to come figure out how to get information off her laptop, and she had a coaching call with me because of a meeting later that day about an important job opportunity—all at the same time. When I got on the phone with her, she was incredibly frustrated.

She'd worked all night on the presentation and woke up to a laptop that wouldn't start and an IT department that wouldn't respond. I don't care if you're superhuman—that feels stressful. You want to punch something. You don't know whether to cry or to break the laptop over your knee. You're in a low state of mind without access to a lot of creative thinking or future-forward thinking. Your brain is dominated by the state of mind that you're in. So, even when it's completely unplanned, you've got to figure out how to reorganize your day to maintain high performance in the things that matter most.

I asked her, "Is there any way that the late afternoon meeting can be postponed? To walk in there in a low state of mind would be unfortunate. You're not going to be at your best, and that's an important conversation."

She told me she actually hadn't thought of that but that it might be okay to move it. She called this executive's admin assistant, and it was a simple switch to the next day. Moving the high-pressure conversation to the following day gave her some space to focus on the problem she was trying to solve.

THE POWER OF PRESENCE

Now, in the example of Stella, if she couldn't move the meeting that day, we would have needed to get more creative. When working with executives who feel like they don't have much flexibility, I love to challenge them to re-think how they spend the three minutes just prior to a big meeting to mentally prepare and "clear" their emotional real estate. In a recent session with a client who was going into a big interview, she planned to mentally prepare. She did one minute of quiet (set timer and close eyes), one minute of focused thought on the best outcome for the meeting ahead, and one minute focused on a few of her strengths that she could rely on to be successful in this meeting. My client reported back that she was amazed that in just three minutes she was able to shift her "game day" readiness so much.

Though we so often think about external busyness as the culprit and cause of stress and overwhelm, by now you should know that this is a mind game more than anything. If you feel caught up in your thoughts, that's a sign you're using up too much of your emotional real estate. When you're feeling internal pressure mounting, you can work to bring some of the present moment back into your life.

For a powerful way to reset, take just one to ten minutes to experience true mindfulness during a mindless activity. As always, start small. When you walk over to the coffee stand, can you become more aware and quiet your mind? When you are driving or stuck in traffic, can you create a shift? How many times do we use up emotional real estate mentally fighting traffic? "Hurry up! Don't turn that way. Oh my God, why are you—what are you doing? Why did you—no blinker? What's *wrong* with you?!" We're using our finite emotional energy on something as meaningless as someone forgetting to put on their blinker. A blinker! That's not a good use of energy. Instead, try to take that time to be completely present. Work to be calm and at peace with what's happening in the moment without letting your mind drift to work or family or thoughts about the world outside of your car.

One client said her aha moment occurred when she finally started to use her time *in traffic* to prepare herself energetically for an important meeting. She said, "The other day I used the full thirty-two-minute drive to become incredibly quiet and present. No radio, no distractions, just the sound of the blinker and an observer point of view of what was happening all around me. I took in the storefronts and became curious about the drivers passing by. I could have spent it thinking about being rushed and impatient, or how frustrating life is and how slow things move. But if that's where my mindset had gone, I would have taken my frustration into the meeting. I couldn't risk that for this meeting, so I chose to trick my brain into thinking that there was very little to worry about." Next traffic jam, give it a shot—what do you have to lose?

EXERCISE #4: THE SEVEN-MINUTE MORNING

You can make real changes to your emotional real estate and state of mind by starting with this short, simple practice. Plan five to seven minutes alone in the morning. Take your cup of coffee and hide in your favorite spot, like a reading chair. If the kids/dog/spouse/roommates are too distracting, book off the first fifteen minutes in your office. For example, I know that if I can get to my office with my coffee before 8:45 a.m., I'll have fifteen minutes to do my routine in peace and plan my day before my first calls start.

If you have to, you can get creative and do the routine on a commute, even on a train or on the subway. Talk through these ideas while you're driving, using the voice memo app on your phone to capture your thoughts. It doesn't have to be on paper; all you need to do is go through the thought process. I prefer to journal mine, but there's no wrong way to build this into your day.

It's about building something repeatable that you use over and over again to help you practice a new way of thinking about your day, your instincts, and your emotional real estate. Use your phone or a timer so you can fully immerse in the task without checking the time.

- **Minute 1: Silence.** In the first minute, get quiet. Become present. Don't look at your timer. This allows you to sit back, close your eyes, and have one full minute of silence. It will feel long but see if you can get comfortable with the quiet. Lengthen this as you build up some meditation muscles, but for today, one minute is all you need.

- **Minute 2: Moments to Savor.** Ask yourself: what are your highlights or favorite moments from the last twenty-four hours? When you bring a zoom lens to the best parts of your day each day, you start to enjoy those moments even more when they happen (you're thinking, "Oh *this* will be my best moment tomorrow during my seven-minute routine for sure!).

- **Minute 3: Emotional Real Estate Check.** Now that we are in a calm and high state of mind, what are the biggest things using up emotional real estate right now? What thoughts do I keep having? What things am I worried about? Get those out on paper. Even exciting things can use up energy. Just jot down what's using your energy right now.

- **Minute 4: Empowering Belief.** Identify the empowering beliefs and affirmations that you need to remind yourself of today. For example: if you are worried about an issue with your spouse, you might decide "I am thankful for this person and I will choose to act out of love today" is your affirmation. If you are waiting to hear back on a big job, you might choose "I know my next great job is out there, whether it's this one or the next."

- **Minute 5: Envision Your Great Day.** Ask yourself, what will you do today to create more emotional real estate for yourself? And what would make today great? Not good, but great. For example, not just surviving a meeting but clearly getting your point across on a big issue. Or, not just having dinner with your kids but feeling like you really got quality time with them tonight. Visualize what that would look like. This practice can make the difference between having a wonderful day and simply surviving.

- **Minute 6: Action.** Think through any final thoughts on what actions you need to take today to make it great and feel you are managing your emotional real estate in an amazing way. Make a couple of notes about tasks that are on your mind or capture notes on ideas that bubble to the surface.

- **Minute 7: Brain Candy.** This last step is devoted to *brain candy*. Take a break to enjoy a quick clip from a book, a quick blog you enjoy, or to pick out a song that you need to listen to. Spend a second massaging in an essential oil to help revitalize your senses. Something that feels sweet to your brain—i.e., Brain Candy.

Some people do stretch this out into fifteen to twenty minutes, but be careful—the longer the routine, the less likely you are to do it every day. The magic here is in creating a habit that you build into your day that raises your state of mind and helps you gain clarity and insight into your emotional real estate.

CHAPTER SIX

Take out the Trash

Learn to say "I hope that works out for you" rather than try to change or fix people.

—MARYAM HASNAA

When you can't change someone or forgive someone, pray for them. It may or may not change them. But it will always change you.

—UNKNOWN

After you've cleaned up your day to make really good use of your energy, you'll have a little bit more space to start thinking beyond the small things. For a while, that will be enough. But eventually, pushing pebbles around the property won't be enough, and that big boulder in front of the window will have to be taken care of. In the next few chapters, we're going to work on those boulders—the bigger concerns taking up space on your emotional real estate.

Some of this stuff is going to require much more attention. Whether it's a bad boss, a challenging marriage, trouble at home, baggage from the past—these are the things that will either require some kind of action, which we'll talk about in the next chapter, or they'll need to be let go.

Remember, the goal is to always have enough free space set aside so we can breathe. Everything that's on our front lawn is piled up in between us and being present. So, if you're lacking space, letting go becomes an important practice. Because when we do that work to clear baggage and let go of it for good, it frees up more than just breathing room. We start to discover space that we often didn't even know was accessible. We feel lighter, freer, and able to focus on the opportunities in front of us.

Let's take it out of the abstract for a second and just think about how good it feels to have a clean house. That feeling comes from more than a sense of accomplishment or that fresh lemon or pine smell. Almost anyone with a clean, decluttered house will say, "I *feel* so much lighter!"

Marie Kondo struck a bestselling chord in *The Life-Changing Magic of Tidying Up* when she asked her readers to declutter by holding each item in their hand, examining it, and only keeping what is useful or brings joy. She understood that if we aren't happy with our lives, none of the other reasoning matters. Anything outside of that she considered clutter and in the way of a clean, tidy house that serves *us* instead of us feeling tied down to it. So why is it so refreshing to let go? Because it's not only the physical burden of a mess that you've cleaned up, but a mental load that you've lifted as well. It's cleansing. Letting go isn't passive—it's actively and intentionally making peace with something so you're no longer holding onto it.

When we look at the things filling up emotional real estate and decide to let go, it's not unlike decluttering. It's possibly the most rewarding step of this process, just as much as getting rid of a ton of junk in your house or on the front lawn would be. Of course, it's one thing to tell someone how great it is to "just let go" and quite another to actually let go. That's okay. This is your emotional real estate and your own process. You can even choose to hang onto something. I'm not going to spend this chapter convincing you to let go of something that you don't think you should let go of. Just understand that whatever you keep is going to continue to take up emotional real estate.

In fact, every single thing that you hold onto comes at the expense of your emotional real estate. Recognizing that truth inspires us to ask, "What *can* I get rid of?" When we identify things we don't have to hold onto, we can choose to take necessary actions to remove them—or, when we're ready, choose to let them go. Letting go and taking action aren't mutually exclusive, either. In fact, one often leads to the other.

When you reach that point where you're ready to let go, you know that it takes more than just tossing that idea out the window. It's time to roll up our sleeves and get to work. We have some garbage to sort through.

KNOW WHEN TO HOLD 'EM

When you realize your emotional real estate is completely consumed, it's tempting to make a big change to help solve the problem because it seems like eliminating a serious obligation or concern would be so freeing (anyone ever commit to quitting their job after a terrible day at work?!). But I want to be really clear about this: when you are in a low state of mind, it will feel nearly impossible to let something go. Instead of an empowered decision to make peace with a thought or memory, when we're in a low state of mind, it's more like throwing our hands in the air in apathy or letting something go with an undertone of spite and a smidgen of grudge.

There's an art to doing nothing—to sitting with what we're feeling instead of pushing toward some kind of response. When we're in a low state of mind over something and feeling frustrated with our options, doing nothing at all is the best choice we can make. In fact, I encourage the people I work with to *savor* their lows.

One of my clients spent four years in a job she didn't love in the effort to position herself for a leadership role in the organization, only to not be selected during the hiring process. The day she found out she didn't get the job, instead of sitting down and having a good cry over all she'd invested in this organization for no apparent reason, she called me within an hour of getting the news.

She said, "I've got to figure out what I'm going to do next. Do you have time to talk tonight?" After we talked, however, I encouraged her to let the sadness soak in a little bit rather than figuring out the next steps just yet. She didn't need to start planning the next move five minutes after getting the bad news. She could give herself permission to take two or three days to just immerse herself in the gap between what she thought would happen and what actually did.

Bridging that gap can be exhausting, but experiencing disappointment is part of being ambitious and chasing things. She played the game hard. I love and admire that in her. Her tendency was to pick herself up and brush herself off, which makes her resilient. She doesn't just wait for things to happen. There is deep wisdom in being able to say, "I've worked hard for something better than this, and I'm feeling frustrated because I didn't expect this to happen." As we've seen over and over throughout this process, awareness alone can do a lot of good. But once we become aware, we don't have to reframe it right away or stuff it down and move along. If I'd only been trained in NLP, that might have been where I stopped. Buddhists would say that suffering is part of the human experience, and they practice meditating and breathing through it. When we're focused on emotional real estate, work-life wisdom demonstrates that it's okay to feel the impact of disappointment. It's good to sit with it. And when it's time to move forward, we can then bring empowering thoughts to our day to help.

Too many times, we think, "Well, that didn't work out. Probably the next thing won't either." Assigning that meaning to a disappointment can feel safer. It absolves us from putting ourselves in a similar situation again. We're better served by drawing a different moral from the story. Instead of hurrying the process along—looking back for meaning or forward for the next thing—celebrate it all as part of the game of life. The emotions that we experience on all rungs of the state of mind ladder are part of the human experience. There's no reason to rush out of them, and we're certainly not benefitted by stuffing them.

Sometimes you will still need to let go in a big way—quit the job or leave the marriage—but I'm suggesting that you can make that decision from an empowered place. Letting go can only really happen from a high state of mind. Start by experiencing that moment for what it is, and then move forward with action or choosing to let go when you're in a higher state of mind. When you've created some space and moved to a higher state of mind, you'll have better control over smarter, more empowered management of your emotional real estate.

KNOW WHEN TO FOLD 'EM

The perception of stress and being too busy to be happy is happening in our thoughts and our mindset, which means it's the stories we're telling ourselves—our limiting beliefs—that keep us stuck. Often, it's not that we *can't* let go, but that a limiting belief prevents us from choosing to let go.

For example, Jim might have just completely embarrassed you in a meeting. What he said was wrong, and it was really hurtful and frustrating, and he said it right in front of your boss. Now you're wondering what people think, why he said it, and how it's going to impact you later.

We can say "let it go" all day long, but that's like saying, "Whatever you do, don't think about an elephant." What's going to happen? You won't be able to get the image of an elephant out of your head! The brain doesn't know how to *not* think about something. So, letting go doesn't mean "stop thinking about it." That's not really possible. Instead, we learn to let go by shifting that story in our minds to an empowering belief.

In the example with Jim, you might be able to hold onto a more empowering belief about that meeting and your role. You might say, "I'm very proud of the work that I'm doing, and I'm going to stand by the fact that I'm working hard and doing a great job. I'm going to stand by my boss telling me he's impressed with the work that I'm doing. I'm going to stand by the fact that Jim didn't understand the full context of the story. I'm going to stand by my ability to make great decisions on this project."

We can create empowering beliefs about anything—not just letting go—but this is where it really shines. It's not easy, necessarily. We can get stuck in negative loops, like, "Jim embarrassed me. I'm so stupid for letting that happen..." But that's why we're looking specifically for *empowering* beliefs. Even if Jim was 100 percent right in what he said, we can create an empowering belief without lying to ourselves about the situation. Find something that's true that you want to amplify.

Letting go isn't passively stuffing your feelings about a situation or telling yourself a lie about the situation you're in. It's an active process.

If I were working with you one-on-one and we reached this point of the journey where you're feeling stuck and hesitant about letting something go, I'd ask you to pick just one thing. You're not actually going to do anything with it yet—just pick one thing on your emotional real estate and visualize letting it go. Look closer than just the surface of it—what is it that you're actually envisioning letting go? For example, if you're thinking about needing permission to do something in the future that's different from what you want to do now, maybe you're actually letting go of your ego and the belief that you need to be God's gift to your industry.

Once we figured out what you were letting go of, I'd ask you to picture it really thoroughly. What would that look like? What fear or emotions are you feeling? What's scary about that idea? What's empowering about it?

Get honest with yourself about what's actually on your emotional real estate, look for an empowering belief about it, then choose to hang onto and nurture that empowering belief rather than the fear and limiting beliefs that have kept those boulders planted firmly on the front lawn.

When we choose an empowering belief—you can do this, you're able to make it through, you can get to the other side—it frees up emotional real estate all on its own, and it also empowers us to take the next steps to actively let things go and free up even more room to breathe. Just like the feeling of a nice, clean, decluttered house, we know we've finally let go of something when we start to feel lighter.

FULLY ACCEPTING WHAT IS

If you were to expect a cat to bark, you'd be rather surprised when it doesn't. If you believed it absolutely *should* bark and that *you* needed to make it happen, that belief would use up a lot of unnecessary emotional real estate. Our own expectations are sometimes the biggest thieves of emotional real estate. Sometimes we set expectations on people and situations that are pretty specific, then they can't live up to the expectations we have of them in our mind. Byron Katie likes to call it the difference between "arguing with reality" and "loving what is."

Instead, we have to learn to look at the proverbial cat without expectation. Whatever comes out of its mouth will be fine with us. We don't need to spend emotional real estate being appalled that the cat won't bark. We don't feel that we have to convince it to try to bark.

Learning to "love what is" and to let those wayward expectations go can change everything. We don't have to be frustrated when our partners or kids or colleagues do something different from what we expected. They are on their own journey and are going to do what they're going to do anyway. When you realize it's not their job to think like you, and it's not your job to make them, you will free up a whole bunch of emotional real estate.

That's not to say there won't be good reasons to try to influence people throughout our lives, but it pays to be mindful about how much emotional real estate we are investing in the process. If everyone is sitting around a table discussing political beliefs, and no one is open to being persuaded by another point of view, what is the point of arguing and using piles of emotional real estate? Honoring that people and perspectives are different, we can still share our views and acknowledge their views and become conscious of not investing our emotional real estate into the discussion or a desire to change someone else's mind.

Whatever is happening in this very moment is your own experience. Arguing with reality creates huge amounts of stress, anxiety, and misery. Sometimes, letting go of those expectations does the trick and you can free up some emotional real estate just like that. Other times, as we learned in the last chapter, you might need to give yourself permission to take a little bit of time before taking trash out to the curb.

Whatever the case, you'll make the wisest choice for you if

you can clearly see and love the world as it is. That means loving that the guy in the office keeps stealing your yogurt to loving the sound of the neighbor's dog barking in the middle of your blissful sleep. You don't have to build a story about reality that is a lie. We don't always have control of our circumstances, but we always have a choice in the way we experience things. When we can love what *is*, we free our emotional real estate and eliminate our need to complain about people, places, and situations.

LETTING GO OF EGO

Letting go doesn't mean you have to agree with or bless the other person's bad behavior, but it does mean you can stop arguing with them in your mind in honor of *your* emotional real estate. All too often, we get locked into a conflict where we want to prove someone wrong. We know it isn't serving anyone, but we don't want to acquiesce, either—so the battle rages on. Let it go. Take it to the curb with the rest of the garbage that's been weighing you down.

Kabbalists view these kinds of arguments and conflicts as centered on ego. Remember, the belief is that at any point in time we're either connected to light and a higher power, or to ego. Light is the desire to receive for the sake of sharing, and ego is the desire to receive for the sake of self. The goal is to always align to something bigger, though the Kabbalist view of the human experience is that we're always fighting this battle in our minds.

Though hanging onto conflicts can seem to be self-protective and that you're holding ground for yourself, ask yourself what part of that is ego talking (reminder: ego speaks up to help *you* get something *you* want).

This awareness is freeing, because we don't have to take those ego-dominant thoughts so seriously. It becomes easier to spot when we're holding onto something for the wrong reasons, which makes it easier to let go. When we let those constant fights go, it is freeing both for ourselves and for the other person.

THE BELL CURVE OF APPROVAL

Interpersonal relationships can take up a lot of emotional real estate, and our beliefs and expectations about them are a big reason why. The skills we're learning for letting go—creating empowering beliefs and accepting the reality of our situation—are important for relationships, and they culminate into the bell curve of approval.

Here's what I've observed after years of working with large groups of people: about 20 percent of the people in any group will approve of you no matter what you do or how you perform. Approximately 60 percent are probably open to what you have to say and will judge you as "okay" or "pretty good" but will have critiques. The remaining 20 percent simply won't ever approve of what you're doing—they just don't get you. That's the bell curve of approval.

When we find out that someone doesn't approve of something we've done, it triggers our ego. We get all sorts of wound up about it, because the ego has gotten involved and wants to take over. The bell curve of approval stands back at 80,000 feet to look at the big picture, which is this: no matter how fabulous you are, you're never going to have a 100 percent approval rating. As clear and reliable as the physics of gravity, the physics of the bell curve of approval assures us that no one is going to have complete acceptance and approval from everyone all of the time.

Yet somewhere in our DNA, we were taught to seek complete approval from everyone. Unfortunately, in order to contort ourselves into perfection and seek approval from everyone, we invariably become inauthentic, which again, uses up emotional real estate. So now we're using up emotional real estate either trying to gain approval, and/or on the inauthenticity, and then we'll use more on the people we upset who had been happy with us in the first place! It's a cyclical dilemma, and when we're stuck in it, it's exhausting.

Far too often, I see ambitious, high-potential professionals using too much emotional real estate in the fear of being judged by somebody who is already a harsh critic. In one of the larger classes that I've taught, there were about twenty-five executives in the room and another facilitator who was there for training. Halfway through the class, we reached an exercise where I would pair people up and ask them to share information about their personal values.

One woman in the class became visibly upset. I watched her roll her eyes and sigh, getting more and more worked up as we discussed the exercise until she finally just got up and walked out.

After I got everyone settled into the exercise, I caught her in the hallway. I asked her, "Hey, I just want to find out—is there anything I did that offended you that I need to be aware of?"

She said, "Honestly, it's not you personally. This exercise really frustrates me. I'm an analytical type of person and would have preferred to do my homework in advance. I don't feel comfortable talking about myself with my colleagues in this way."

Fair enough. I told her that she could call me if I could do anything to be of better service, but since this was the design of the course, I would fully understand if she chose to step out.

I went back into the room after that and taught the rest of the course without any problems. Afterward, the facilitator who I was training told me she couldn't believe how well I handled the woman who left. She said I didn't even look phased.

Since you've been with me since the beginning of my story now, you know that the old version of me certainly would have been phased. I would have dropped everything—all of the people who were completely happy in the room—and would have been distracted and distressed about the one unhappy person in the room. But she was at the bottom 20 percent of my bell curve. I know now that there's nothing I can do to avoid that. I can't change my style to make her happy. If I did that, I would just make someone else miserable. I would wreck my confidence and ruin my own authenticity.

I often get coaching clients who come in frustrated stating that someone is constantly critiquing them for their presentation skills, and you can quickly spot them using inordinate amounts of emotional real estate seeking that elusive approval, resulting in less energy for everything else. But the minute that we completely acknowledge and accept the fact that other people are not going to change, and that certain people are simply going to come from a different place, our load lightens.

On the other hand, just because someone is in your bottom 20 percent does not mean that their critiques hold no value. Instead of getting caught up in personal disappointment, drill into the useful piece of feedback that someone might be offering and toss the rest.

In addition, we *can* learn a lot from our bottom 20 percent. I was working with a client who, after many sessions focused on her boss's approval, finally agreed she was never going to hear her boss say, "You're the best person I've ever worked with and I really think you're amazing, Jane." When she finally felt life was going to be okay without hearing that, she said she felt lighter because the fight to get that approval was over. She also felt it became easier for her to take a few useful points he has made into consideration as she works to improve. The minute we can disconnect from that and zoom in on what might be valuable, the better off we are.

So many powerful executives I know fight to get approval from the bottom 20 percent and tend to act completely different than who they really are. They go home stressed at night because they've spent the day biting their lip or trying too hard to make that person happy. Then they wake up the next day with the stress of wondering whether that person will approve of their next presentation or project. Focusing here clouds our ability to access good information. All that energy is lost on trying to solve a problem that can't be solved.

Bring focus to the relationships that fuel our emotional real estate, since they are in our top 20 percent. With them, we feel supported, empowered, and loved. When you look at your bell curve of approval, it's clear that you can't make everyone happy. You just can't. And it feels amazing to stop trying.

When one person's dissatisfaction is driving you crazy, or you're struggling with self-confidence in a situation where you're feeling judged by a lot of people, remember that bell curve of approval. The more that you use it, the easier those situations become.

"I WANT TO BE YOUR BUS DRIVER"

Around the time I was launching my business, I had plenty of detractors who were squarely in my bottom 20 percent. It wasn't so much that they didn't approve of me, but they really couldn't understand how I expected to make it without a million-dollar idea or without more experience, and on top of it, the economy was at an all-time worst. So, I leaned heavily on a trusted friend and mentor, who was on the opposite end of the curve. He kept reassuring me, "I know you. I know how smart you are and how passionate you are about helping people. If you just focus on this, there's no way you can't be successful. If you could see what I see, you'd know that it's not possible for you to fail. Just stay focused."

He was so sure I would be a wild success, he would joke about my future being so bright that one day I would be asked to take a speaking tour by bus over North America to share my secrets of success. He'd tell me, "I just hope one day when you are a big deal, you'll let me be your bus driver." And with that, I nicknamed him "the bus driver."

I didn't have many empowering beliefs of my own, but my future bus driver was insistent: success was inevitable if I just stayed focused. He was adamant about not letting me use up emotional real estate whining about the economy, chasing job offers to try to "save myself from trying to start a business." He insisted that I channel all my emotional real estate into making my dream happen. I could become successful, but not if I watered down my emotional real estate trying to take a bunch of odd jobs; I wouldn't have enough to make it happen.

He was so convinced, that I began to believe him. He trusted that he knew what successful people were all about, and I felt less stressed and fearful seeing things from his perspective. At some point in our lives, we will need to lean on those top 20 percent, cheerleading bus drivers who just want to see us win. If you can't find your own empowering belief, go ask your bus driver.

BE YOUR OWN BUS DRIVER

Some detractors are easier to make peace with than others. There are things in our past, and some in our present, that we can't resolve with the other person. That might be the case for any number of reasons, and often our response is to simply hang onto those things. If you can lift yourself out of those spaces—away from the unresolved conflicts and out of the day-to-day stress—and focus on the bigger picture, that baggage can finally be moved off of your real estate for good.

The Christmas before my big breakup, I had put all my energy into making Christmas perfect for my boyfriend's ten-year-old daughter. I'd wrapped presents all night, and I had invited his parents for dinner. I tried so hard to make it perfect. Then, Christmas morning, something stupid happened and, before I knew it, he had lost his patience and was yelling at me. No "thank you" for the effort at all—just a needling criticism of some small oversight. It was infuriating.

I remember running out to the store, driving alone in my car, so angry, hurt, and bawling. I tried to let it go, but it was just so upsetting that I couldn't shake it. But it was the holidays, and I didn't want to ruin them by being in a miserable state of mind. So, in that moment, I remember thinking, "What is it that my ego needs to hear? What is it that I wanted him to say to me this morning?"

So, alone in my car, I started to speak out loud the words I was hoping he would say. I imagined him realizing he hadn't told me how much he appreciated me. In my mind, I had him say thank you to me for driving to three different stores to get the right gifts and make sure we had wrapping paper. Before long, I was saying the words I needed to hear, out loud to myself in the car. "Christine, I'm so thankful that you put all this energy into the holiday. I'm so impressed with how you went out of your way to make this holiday special for not just me and my daughter, but for my parents, too. Thank you."

This was an emotional moment for me. I realized that I hadn't been hearing these things from him, and I'd been so upset while waiting and hoping to hear them. He wasn't ever going to say them, so I had to affirm myself and give myself what I needed in that moment. I had to become my own bus driver. Sound familiar?

Less than a month later, I made the bold decision to leave this relationship. I realized that, although I could see many great reasons to stay, I was using up so much emotional real estate each day in the attempt to gain approval from someone else. And although I knew I wouldn't get that approval, somehow, I thought I could live without it. Thankfully, I eventually realized that this relationship ran a deficit, instead of generating a return. And ironically, within a week of moving out on my own, although I was still very sad, I started to feel like I finally had more emotional real estate free—for me—because nothing was taxing me. I had more peace. I remember hanging out alone on a Friday night enjoying a movie and a glass of wine thinking, "Hey, you. You're actually a lot of fun to hang out with—where have you been?!"

We continually use up emotional real estate on our detractors, running the tapes that they play for us and holding onto the hurt. It can get really difficult to let go of them. But if you can reverse engineer the situation and give yourself the affirmation you need to feel loved and valued, it can change the energy of those wounds and how you approach them mentally.

Your subconscious needs are probably different from mine. I needed acknowledgment. You might need to be told you are the smartest person in the room, or the most loving. When others fail to give us those messages and we decide to get frustrated, we start using up emotional real estate.

The question then becomes: What should I be saying to

myself more often instead of waiting for someone else to say it to me? Or, do I believe it without somebody else validating it?

"LET GO" LIST

It takes a tremendous amount of mental muscle to let hurts and disappointment go when there is no proper closure or an apology. You can make it easier by practicing: write out the things you've effectively let go of without that apology or closure.

My "let go" list includes mistakes that were made in the hospital when I gave birth to my daughter and sexual harassment in the workplace when the guy wasn't fired afterward. It also identifies smaller conflicts, like when we tried to cut down a tree in our yard and it turned into a giant dispute with our neighbor. It would have been easy to continue harping on my belief that my neighbor was wrong and owed us an apology but holding space for that grudge didn't feel like a good use of emotional real estate. I decided to continue to build a good relationship with my neighbor regardless of how strongly I disagreed with them. Now, our relationship has moved into a great space.

Sometimes, people get scared of letting go because they're afraid that means they're endorsing bad beliefs or bad behavior. You can identify wrongdoing and still let go. You can understand that no, a neighbor should not borrow a lawn mower and not return it, but if that behavior continues to use a lot of your emotional real estate long after the moment is over, you might choose not to feed that grudge.

If you can recognize those moments that you chose to let go—big or small—and realize the benefit that came from that choice, you'll be encouraged to do the same in the future. Looking at your "let go" list, you might find that most of the things you were once so worried about truly don't matter anymore. Reading down your list also gives you a sense of accomplishment and encourages you to try it again.

EXERCISE #5: FIFTEEN WAYS TO LET GO

Now that we've become aware of negative thoughts that bombard your mind, it is time to let them go. Still, the concept of "letting go" can feel vague in practice. Here are fifteen practical ways to let go of something when you are convinced you can't. For this exercise, just choose one item you've been struggling with and apply one or more of these strategies to it. Write down the negative thought and explain why it's time to let it go, referencing any of the concepts below.

1. In a high state of mind, decide it's time to forgive someone—either yourself or someone else. Do it because it gives back emotional real estate.

2. Notice whether you had an expectation of a person or situation and not an agreement.

3. Contemplate how forgiving does not mean that you must condone or agree with what someone did—it means you are willing to free yourself and stop using emotional real estate to keep the story alive in your head of what they did wrong.

4. Find empathy for someone you feel judgment towards.

5. Let the universe work its magic—choose something that bothers you and make the conscious decision to leave it for something bigger to solve (Universe, God, Source, Spirit, Allah, Buddha, alien leaders from outer space).

6. Give yourself permission to never understand why something happened. See what that does for your emotional real estate.

7. See if you can find a situation in which you are using lots of judgment. Try to picture what questions a curious mind might ask about this situation.

8. List five reasons why this outcome could be exactly how life intended it to be and this experience is ultimately for your benefit.

9. Although something has upset you today, list five angry thoughts you have right now that you may one day choose to forget or let go.

10. Play third person; pretend you don't know the whole story. What pieces of the story could you be missing? Pretend you just learned something new. How would it change if there were pieces missing?

11. Honor the fact that each person is doing their best given what they are capable, even if it doesn't match with what your best would be.

12. Choose an empowering thought to repeat to yourself right now. Find one that raises your state of mind.

13. Notice where your ego is damaged—remind your ego it doesn't have to be right or get its way all the time.

14. Be thankful for the whole experience of life, including the full range of experiences from joy to pain; as my grandfather once said, "You are just a spirit having a human experience."

15. Commit to fully loving the present moment, bringing all your attention to this exact moment—here is where you have control. Notice what each of your five senses are experiencing. Focus here. Now.

CHAPTER SEVEN

Landscaping

When thinking about life remember this: no amount of regret can solve the past and no amount of anxiety can change the future.

—UNKNOWN

Not everything is as easy as letting go or rearranging your day. Those unspoken conflicts, unattended and ignored, don't go away. They only grow and continue to take up emotional real estate until we intentionally remove them. Especially with interpersonal issues, if that tension is changing the way you work and interact with someone and you try to let it slide, you'll miss an opportunity to gain clarity. Sometimes, it's important to take action on something that's taking up emotional real estate so you can let the rest of the thinking about it go.

Not long ago, I was in a meeting with a peer, and it felt like she snapped at me. I left that meeting feeling we were no longer on great working terms. As I had dinner that night, it was on my mind. Late at night as I was heading to bed, it was still there. I knew that I would have to take action in order to free up space. The next day I shot her a note requesting a quick call. Secretly I was very nervous. On our call, I said, "When we worked together in the past, everything went really well. For some reason, I'm sensing that things are not as good as they used to be. Something has gone sideways here. What do you think?"

That brief introduction opened the door for a meaningful conversation. She didn't realize I'd felt that way, but she was also candid about how she saw some of the work challenges we are facing. As soon as we got on the same page, we were both able to share how much we loved working with each other, and she was glad that I called to work it out. As I hung up the phone, I felt lighter. Without that conversation, that circumstance could have boiled under the surface indefinitely. Remember, sometimes it's better to take action, because it's good for *our own* emotional real estate.

Let's also be clear: it's not really possible to be free and clear of all thinking and thoughts. Some things need to take up space. Parenting requires emotional real estate to raise children and to keep them healthy. Sick family, career, and relationships require ongoing commitment and care. Money issues tend to use up a lot of space. Everyday life uses up lots of emotional real estate. If not mindfully managed, every bit of it will be claimed by someone or something. Because emotional real estate is finite, you'll need to identify what needs to stay and what can slip down the list for now; set them aside and gain some space to take care of yourself in the way that you need.

Remember, stress happens when you *perceive* that the load of energy required to make everything happen is greater than what you have available. The paradigm of emotional real estate helps us to know exactly what we have available, what can be eliminated, and how we can adjust our mindset and lives to create more space. It's time to reorganize your emotional real estate so you're ready to deal with the surprises, changes, and struggles each day brings. This is where we begin to landscape, making your emotional real estate look more like what we want for the long term.

The beautiful thing about landscaping your emotional real estate—taking action—is that *you* get to make the decisions. Here are a few important ideas to keep in mind:

- You're going to make conscious choices. Sometimes you have to take action, sometimes you let go. Sometimes you take one small action so you can let the rest of the issue go. These two concepts work together to help you free up space.

- Just having the action plan itself can free up emotional real estate. For example, if you are worried sick about your child's situation at school with a bad teacher, you might decide to reach out and arrange a meeting with the teacher to understand his perspective. So for now, you can stop worrying and go back to being present.
- Take action where you have influence. Since we can't change everything that drives us crazy, it's the best use of emotional real estate to focus on what you can influence. If you can't change the teacher, consider how you can influence your child in working through the situation or how you can work with the school to address the issue. If you are up at night worrying, start to brainstorm where you have influence.
- Procrastination takes up a lot of emotional real estate. A lot. Oftentimes, more than taking action does. If you are debating over whether to go to that yoga class tonight and you know if you don't, you'll spend two hours beating yourself up over not going, consider grabbing the mat and walking out the door before your mind has time to object.

LOSE A DIFFERENT WAY

Think about your bathtub plumbing. If you're consistently getting cold water every day and you want to get warm water, you have to make a change to the current system. Once you've made a change, you can run the water and assess whether you're going to get a different result. This is a powerful way to solve a lot of really big problems: map the current system, find the flaws in it, then map the new system. With a new map, what steps are you going to focus on changing? As soon as you turn it into an experiment, you can relax a little; you don't have to worry about getting the right result. Just see what happens when you change *something*.

I learned this from a guy I was seated next to on a flight, who asked me what I do. I told him I was a management consultant, and he was interested in my work. I told him, "The challenge is, even if you fix the business, if the leadership doesn't see anything as different, the business goes back to acting the exact same way again after you leave. That's the challenge with my job."

He said, "That's funny, because I'm a child psychologist and I have the exact same problem. I can help a child to see the world differently, but if the parents don't change, the child will run into the same problems again and again." He said that his dad's favorite phrase had been, "Try to lose a different way."

I was so inspired by that, I took it back to my team. "We're trying our hardest and we're falling down on our faces.

Our new mission statement is *try to lose a different way*. Whatever we do, we're going to do it differently to see if we can get a different result." The spirit of experimentation encourages us to think differently about those recurring issues. It shifts our perspective from judgmental or frustrated to curious. Since we know that state of mind affects the way we're using emotional real estate when we're struggling with something, this has a huge impact on how we can make the change.

BREAK THE PERFECT SYSTEM

If you've found yourself in a *Groundhog Day* situation, facing burnout after burnout, congratulations! You've created a system that's repeatable. You're an excellent engineer who understands that belief drives action, which drives belief, which drives a new action, which ultimately gets a result, and then the whole system repeats itself again.

Sometimes that's what we want—predictable results. But other times, it's not. When we keep getting the wrong results, we often feel helpless to change it. You might find yourself saying, "I don't know why, but I always go to work for bad bosses..." or date the wrong partners, or make the wrong friends, or whatever it might be. That's okay. Recognize the benefit of doing something repeatable and acknowledge that you've already been able to make that happen.

When one of my coaching clients wanted a new job, I asked her why she was frustrated in her existing job. She said, "This is the third or fourth time it's happened. I always work for these narcissistic, selfish, male-dominated bosses. I keep going to work for the same guy in a different body. Different company, different guy, same situation. I don't even trust myself anymore to go interview for another job. I don't know how to prevent this from happening again."

Okay, great—I applauded her accomplishment as she had created the perfect system for going to work for a narcissistic boss. Cool! (She started laughing about this topic for the first time.) I said, "So can you teach me how to go work for a narcissistic boss? Help me understand the steps."

She told me the first thing to do was to be currently working for a narcissistic boss, and be really, really eager to leave. "Have an incredible urgency to leave because you're really pissed off. You put your feelers out to everybody you know and tell them how eager you are for a move. Then, talk to a bunch of different people who might have positions or openings and see what kind of jobs are available."

She got quiet for a moment, then continued, "Take the first job offer you get after your prospective boss sells you on the fact that you're going to be God's gift to his department."

The steps were clear. Leave the existing job, give them the big middle finger, then go work for someone else who sells you on how awesome you are and swears they will be the greatest boss on the planet.

I told her, "Help me understand. It sounds like when your ego is fed while they're trying to attract you, it helps you make a really fast decision without doing a lot of additional due diligence."

"That's exactly what I do. As soon as I'm told I'd be the greatest thing since sliced bread, I jump on the bandwagon believing that they are going to be the greatest thing since sliced bread. As the months unfold, I discover I've yet again started working for someone narcissistic and selfish. I usually work in that role for sixteen or eighteen months believing if I just work hard enough and sacrifice my personal time and health, I can somehow impress him so he will say those nice things from the interview again. When I realize he's just going to take advantage of me and burn me out, working me to the bone without giving me credit for my work, I finally get fed up and get desperate to leave."

Once we saw the system in action, we could see just what was happening. When stuck in a low state of mind, she would make the decision to leave quickly and pissed off. And then she'd jump to the next position, which was not a better fit.

We started to brainstorm how to break her perfect system. If we were to take just that one piece of the perfect system and swap it out for something different, what would change? Could she try to find a few job offers instead of jumping on the first one? Could she get more clear on what was important to her? Before she accepted any offer, could she talk to other people on the team that work for him? Could she make the effort to work for people who have a great reputation as a boss instead of just working for anybody? Could she reduce the urgency she felt to get out of the existing job and be more mindful before accepting the next one?

The good news is that yes, today she's working for someone she admires deeply, and she's been in that role for over three years now with no desire to leave. But the best part of this story is not only was she happy to report that work was better and she had taken some action to lose some weight, she said she felt she was finally using her emotional real estate on the things that were most important to her.

THE PERFECT SUBCONSCIOUS SYSTEM

Mapping your system can be helpful, but it's good to know that sometimes a coach or therapist can be helpful if you sense there's something bigger to your perfect system you can't identify. For example, I worked with an executive in her fifties who felt incredibly anxious every time any sort of big change was proposed in her company. Her chest would instantly tighten, and she'd feel short of breath, and she didn't know why. She was terrified when she'd been asked to lead a change without instruction, and she found herself always pushing for her team to stay with what felt safe.

During a deep coaching session, I learned that as a young child she had been sent to stay at a boarding school, a change that felt overwhelming and devastating to her. Despite her begging to go home for months, given her parents' situation, she had no choice but to stay and accept this change. Even though the experience ended a few years later, she still carried the scar of that experience with her. Once we realized this, we were able to identify the feeling of anxiety she'd mapped to the experience of change, and help her grow awareness she could use to make a shift.

She learned that although what happened to her as a little girl felt like being attacked by a tiger, what was happening to her over forty years later was more like being handed a kitten. These two experiences were very different, though they shared similarities. Her mind mapped aspects of these situations together, so she experienced both situations like a tiger attack. Soon, when the topic of change came up, she learned to visualize a kitten being gently handed to her to take care of. I challenged her to smile at the kitten and, in her mind's eye, approach it with curiosity and warmth. Once she started to see change more clearly in her consciousness, it was easy for her to re-think her perfect system.

LITTLE HABITS CREATE BIG IMPACTS

Anytime you make a change in your life, you'll use up a lot of emotional real estate. Sometimes, we can do that for a one-time action. But other actions need to happen over and over again, and we can't sustain that much emotional real estate on one thing for long. That makes things like trying to lose weight, quit smoking, and change unwanted behaviors seem like massive boulders on our emotional real estate.

Habit, on the other hand, doesn't require much space at all. Once our brains have been programmed to do the same thing over and over, our subconscious mind kicks into action and we don't have to muster much energy to get it done.

Let me ask you a question that I like to ask during conferences and speaking engagements: is there any chance that you forgot to brush your teeth today? Yeah, I didn't think so. No one in the room at those events forgets to brush their teeth either (or at least they don't admit it).

Let me ask you another question. How are you doing with that New Year's resolution you made? Are you still going to the gym every day?

Whether or not we're aware of it, habit is at play in our lives every single day. The subconscious mind is always at work, making sure things like brushing our teeth happen without having to think about it. As humans, our brains are always trying to get more efficient. When we do things over and over again, our brains adapt to do the work subconsciously. That makes habit a powerful tool that can get a lot of stuff done, and it can make for a really great day.

Think of the mind like a map or a collection of spider webs. The memory of each sight, smell, sound, feeling, and emotion is mapped together when stored in the brain. You don't forget to brush your teeth each morning, because getting up each morning is linked to going to the bathroom, which is linked to standing at the sink reaching for the toothpaste. It's an ingrained habit. This is what NLP helps explain. Mind mapping helps us understand how habits form. Good and bad habits, even addictions, all develop from those spider webs that map information together.

Once you realize how habits work, you can use that power to consolidate some emotional real estate. Create a pattern around something you need to do, do it over and over again, and eventually, the power of habit will kick in and do the heavy lifting for you. Instead of taking on too many changes at the same time, begin by turning one new goal into a habit, map it into your subconscious, and you'll find you have more room to make the next move.

WHY CHANGING HABITS FEELS HARD

Did you ever wonder why it takes so much effort to settle into a new job, even if you're perfectly capable and qualified? That's because everything is new, and you haven't acquired the habits that will make some parts of your day routine. It's not mapped into your subconscious yet. Just logging into your email on the first day can use a lot of emotional real estate. You're thinking, "What's my password again? What's the login? How do I do this? Did I click the wrong button? Please tell me I didn't send this to everyone in the company!" Over time, however, you master those routine parts of the job and can use your time and attention to excel at the role you were hired for.

Even when you know what your next step should be, making change stick can be extremely challenging. As anyone who has ever quit smoking or cut out sweet treats understands, it's hard to give up the satisfaction of the current moment in service to a better future. Human beings are more or less motivated to change based on where they fall on a scale from what's personal, certain, and immediate to what's impersonal, uncertain, and delayed.

We naturally gravitate to activities that give us immediate gratification; if a slice of chocolate cake feels good now, and you're not certain you'll gain ten pounds tomorrow, you'll do what provides personal, certain, and immediate satisfaction. Grab your fork.

To change that habit, it helps to find new ways to map a habit with something that feels just as immediately rewarding. In other words, we can "trick" the subconscious into preferring the healthier behavior if it's equally personal, certain, and immediate. When you want to change a specific behavior, you not only need to replace an old habit with a new one, but you need to practice it until your mind is re-mapped to accept it. Of course, it's easier to commit to practice if you're already getting some reward from the new behavior.

Intentionally building a habit requires training your brain by following the same exact route over and over to establish that new mind map. It's mindfully and consistently recreating the same scenario.

I was recently working with a client who wanted to build a stronger fitness routine into her very busy life. One of the things we discussed is how hard it felt to make that change when she preferred to watch Netflix and scroll Facebook to unwind from her hectic job and crazy kids.

Knowing how the power of habit works, we worked on laying out a routine that could be repeated over and over again to help her subconscious mind kick in so she didn't need to constantly use so much emotional real estate on trying to get fit. We planned out how she'd go to the gym at the same time on the same three days a week, getting into her gym clothes at the same time each day, driving over in the same car, and parking in the same parking spot if possible. We were purposefully helping her brain map this habit so that she had less conscious work to do. When 6:30 a.m. started blinking on the bedside clock, she would know it was time to get into her gear. She'd know where her gym shoes were and that she needed to have them on by 6:40. She'd know when to get in the car to be on time for her 7:00 a.m. class, and as she walked up for class, she'd already know she'd be leaving by 7:50 and hitting the shower by 8:00.

Eventually, when a pattern is repeated (usually, for three to four weeks), the subconscious mind starts to do some of the work, and then it becomes a habit. Once you've built that habit out, you use less emotional real estate thinking about it. When you've truly integrated the habit, even your thought processes can change. Somewhere along the line, my client may find herself *missing* that workout when it doesn't happen. When the mind has re-mapped, she'll now use emotional real estate when she *misses* a workout, and she'll have a new habit that feels like a natural part of her life instead of an obstacle or obligation eating up energy.

The first weeks of any change can be challenging, so this is why we hear time and time again that enlisting an accountability partner to help make a change in habit really helps. For exercise, this looks like a personal trainer, a walking partner, or an energetic puppy who needs to be walked twice a day. These are some of the ways we can start to understand how to design in the creation of new habits as a way to free up energy.

Finally, always remember that you're in the driver's seat. Personally, I currently have about twenty pounds of baby weight to lose. These days, I'm leveraging the power of habit to build some great fitness routines into my week to help me gain energy and feel strong again. But I also have acknowledged that I don't have the emotional real estate available right now, with two children under three at home and a growing business to run, to try specific diet routines or track food. I've decided that for now, building my fitness habit to feel strong and giving myself permission to love my body as is and thanking it for making two beautiful babies is the right focus for me. In the future, I'm sure I'll decide to allocate more emotional real estate to getting focused on dietary changes needed to drop those twenty pounds. Each time we tackle something sitting on our emotional real estate, we can choose to take action, let go, or allow it the space to stay where it's at. Once that becomes our practice, we are owning our own work-life wisdom and can move on to the fun part: creating new space.

EXERCISE #6: LANDSCAPING TOOLS

Now it's time to bring focus to things we do over and over again that are not effective, and to bring attention to how we can create habits that actually serve us rather than hinder us.

- **Perfect System:** Ask yourself what action or belief you can change that would force the system to create different results. Can you draw a process map to show what belief drove an action that created the next belief and the next action? Do you see any flaws in your perfect system?

- **Create a Change of Habit:** Think of something currently sitting on your emotional real estate—maybe a habit of over-eating or sleeping in too late or leaving laundry in the washer overnight— something that just eats at your energy that you'd like to stop doing. Now think of the habit you want to create in place of that. For example, instead of drinking wine in the evenings, can tea take its place? Maybe you want to create a habit of doing the seven-minute routine each morning! Re-map the way that process looks, then take action. Hold your new habit constant for three weeks and see if your brain starts to re-wire itself.

CHAPTER EIGHT

Become an Investor

Live the full life of the mind, exhilarated by new ideas, intox-icated by the romance of the unusual.

—ERNEST HEMINGWAY

The most exciting part of the emotional real estate para-digm is that once you've got the basic landscaping done, it's time to find things that generate *more* energy than they require. It all starts to come together into a practice where we're constantly managing the use of our emotional real estate so that there's always free space available to be happy. Now that we've walked through how to let go or take action on things eating up too much space, we can begin to find what things we can do that provide a return on our investment—what gives back more emotional real estate than it uses up?

Just the other day, I watched this play out with a client of mine, Rosa. She told me about her existing role with her company, and how she'd been in the same spot for a few years now. She really felt like she should be advancing to a senior level position by this point. She was scared her boss felt she didn't want to be promoted anymore. But on the other hand, she also has two challenging teenagers at home, plus a terminally ill mother-in-law, and all of that added to her struggle. She said as much as she wanted to move up, she couldn't get excited about putting in the effort to get a promotion because of everything else. On top of it all, her job itself was very high stress, life with teenagers and illness felt like stress, and she literally had no point in the day where she felt happy.

I asked her to walk me through a typical day, step by step. She'd start at six in the morning trying to get ahead of emails, while soon after trying to get two complaining teenagers up and ready for school—still checking her phone as early emails continued to come in for work. If she didn't get to eat, as soon as the kids were gone, she'd eat something that resembled breakfast, while answering emails, while commuting to work on the crowded rush-hour street car. By nine, she'd walk in the door at work and not stop until five, rarely even pausing for lunch. She'd leave at 5:00 p.m. feeling guilty that she couldn't stay late like her peers. She'd be home by 6:00 p.m., and she'd immediately start making a meal, attempt to sit down for a short dinner, which was enjoyable only if her kids were in an okay mood, and then she'd start cleanup afterward while managing homework and more emails. Most nights she'd fall into bed browsing Facebook until she fell asleep. Weekends were spent doing everything she could for her mother-in-law.

So, we started into a discussion around her work-life wisdom. Where was it at play these days? She was quick to admit she didn't feel like she had any, and if she did, she sure wasn't using it. She laughed about how the term "work-life balance" would frustrate her given she currently felt that both her work and her family each required more than 50 percent of her, and that math still left nothing in there for her. She couldn't separate it out into equal boxes—she was exhausted, and all aspects of her life were calling to her.

Work-life wisdom could put some choices back into her hands. Instead of trying to figure out how to give more, she needed to figure out where to dial back and let go of some of the guilt and expectations she was harboring, like we talked about in chapter six. When we discussed letting go, she knew that her belief that her job was to make her teens "happy" was a falsehood that weighed on her. She also struggled with the belief that if she had more time, they would be happier. We dug into these beliefs to see where she was empowered and where she wasn't. She saw that a more empowering belief would be for her to teach her kids how to be happy instead of being responsible for their happiness. She also realized that their emotions each day were not a reflection of her—and she saw how her "perfect system" was built around her believing it was.

She also realized that she could take a single action with her boss, like we covered in chapter seven. She could talk to her boss about her interest in advancing and help him understand that she needed to stage her own career advancement in parallel with the demands of her family. She knew that in just a few short years, when her kids were through with high school, she would feel more excited about exerting energy in a new role. Meanwhile, she wanted to work with him on a development plan that would help her develop the skills she needed to advance when the time was right.

We also talked about the small stuff, like in chapter five. We talked about going on Facebook at night in a low state of mind, after an evening of fighting with the kids, only to see smiling pictures of her friends' teenagers. In a low state, our brains look for evidence that what's happening in our lives is somehow worse than everyone else's. We hang onto that victim mindset like a badge of honor—that somehow stress is the price we pay for being successful, and that we have no choice but to feel this way. It wasn't mandatory to browse Facebook at night, and it wasn't mandatory for her to check emails all morning. She started to see ways to rearrange small practices to carve out some time for a decent breakfast and a better morning for herself. She also committed to practicing her seven-minute routine on the way to work to help her align her mindset and intentions for the day.

The last thing we talked about is what we're about to cover in this chapter. She decided to incorporate more things into her day and week that would give back emotional real estate, like walking down to the beach with her husband in the evenings. She also started heading to the farmer's market early on Saturdays to get the freshest produce for planning and cooking a special meal on Saturday nights (while ordering pizza for her kids). She told me that just walking outside to get some fresh air every evening helped her feel a quick escape from her busy day. She also said she feels so alive as Saturdays now include the act of cooking and enjoying a meal that is exactly to her liking (and not edited to meet the palate of her fussy teens). The way that Rosa is now managing her emotional real estate is completely integrated into her life and what she needs at this time. It will change, and she'll be ready for it. But in the meantime, she knows exactly how to open up free space and how to invest some time in herself that will create returns in the form of even more free emotional real estate.

WHAT GIVES BACK?

Open Oprah's latest magazine, and you'll undoubtedly see an article titled something like "Five Ways to Reduce Stress." It'll tell you to get to a yoga class, try meditation, pressure cook your favorite dish, and drink a cup of chamomile tea. All good advice, except maybe you're more of a kickboxing type who would rather drink coffee at midnight than sip an herbal concoction at any time of day. What we all really need is the wisdom to know what activities, commitments, and relationships have the largest return on investment for us personally.

Some of these energy boosters might seem to take up even more time at first, but remember that we're not just allocating our time. We're changing mindsets, freeing up mental space, and changing the way our energy is allocated. Emotional real estate operates on simple math—adding actions and subtracting baggage—but this is where we get into exponential returns.

The question isn't what creates more time, but what *restores your energy?* If we spend an hour doing something we love, how much will that free us up to deal with the rest of life? Each of us is unique, so it makes sense that different things will reenergize different people. Don't be fooled into making a list of things you think *should* refresh you. Saying, "I should be doing this" often just makes people feel worse. Stop *shoulding* all over yourself! (I can't find who originally stated this quote, but it's a good one! *We only begin to feel better when we begin to align our thoughts and activities with our instincts to generate more energy.*)

Maybe you gain energy by spending time with others or having a night out with friends. Maybe you're refreshed by taking some time for yourself. For some people, it's as simple as walking the dog in the park, while others need to invest in certain kinds of relationships or a big goal that exists outside of work, like a charity or campaign. When your friend recommends a meditation class, you may think it's a good idea because that's a thing people do to relax, but if you just feel like you're dragging yourself to each session, it's probably not for you. Don't torture yourself by soldiering on or feeling guilty each Monday for making another excuse to not go, wondering why you are so lazy. You don't need to add another activity to your schedule if it's only going to drain your energy.

To find the activities that restore your energy, practice becoming very present and aware of how your energy feels before, during, and after that activity. What does it feel like to do something that gives back more energy than it takes? Notice what you're doing when you get that refreshed feeling, identify those activities as energy boosters, and begin to make time for them—not just once, but as a conscious part of the day, once again leveraging that power of habit.

REVERSE ENGINEERING HAPPINESS

When we train ourselves to look at stress within the framework of emotional real estate, we find new ways to organize our thoughts, obligations, and baggage. It's like a game of Tetris—this can be dropped here, this can be pushed off the edge, and voila, this line can be cleaned up. By bringing awareness to these possibilities, we're training the brain to see ways to repackage and reorganize the components of our lives in order to free up more emotional real estate.

We've now worked on clearing your emotional real estate, reallocating the things that you've kept, and ways to generate even more capacity for yourself. You're in a good place now, able to do what needs doing, without becoming overwhelmed and risking burnout. You might think, "Okay, this is better, but is this all there is?" I don't think it is. I think there's another important layer to emotional real estate, and that's the place where you're no longer too busy to be happy—where you can learn to feed your soul.

I have a client who changed jobs to one that didn't require so many hours, and then moved her family close to the office so she only had a five-minute commute. She chose the job and the house carefully, with the clear intention to get her stress levels under control. But once it was all in place, she felt less stressed but still didn't feel particularly happy, and she couldn't pinpoint why. In fact, she felt bored. She'd created a lot of space—she was no longer using up all her emotional real estate every day keeping up with her commute and long hours—but she wasn't quite done. She had another step to take. She needed to add things to her life that brought her joy.

She had newly freed emotional real estate, but that space was getting used on Netflix, chores around the house, surfing the web, and the odds and ends of life. At the end of the day, she felt less stressed, but not necessarily satisfied. She was happier than she'd been, but she felt certain there was room for more. So, I suggested she look for projects or things that would feed her soul. We had some productive discussions about what might bring joy back into her life, and she surprised herself by turning to music—singing and playing guitar—as she'd done when she was a kid.

The thought of picking up a guitar again after fifteen or twenty years was daunting. She carried a lot of baggage about why she hadn't played. She wasn't talented enough, it had been so many years, it takes too much effort to practice, etc. When we finally decided that it was on her list of things to try, though it took a lot of emotional real estate for her to get started again. If you've ever had the habit of working out and then lost it, you know how difficult it can be to reboot your practice. You tell yourself how it's going to be so hard, you're not going to be good at it, and any other excuse you can find. The only way to get past that mentality is to, as Nike admonishes, "Just do it."

My client took a few weeks to overcome her own thinking enough to pull the guitar out of its box. Finally, she found herself with some free time, and within an hour of first strumming that guitar again, it lit a fire in her to bring back the practice of making music. She later told me, "I'd forgotten how much I like just being completely present with the sounds. Even if my playing doesn't sound like much to others, it's so relaxing and it feels good. It feels indulgent, because it's completely for the sake of my own pleasure. There's no goal-related outcome."

Instead of practicing mindfulness, activities like this naturally bring us back to presence and mindfulness. They don't feel like chores. In fact, it's almost magical. Instead of making a practice out of mindfulness, we can reverse engineer that kind of presence and happiness with a practice that induces mindfulness as an afterthought. Like my client and her guitar, we don't have to do anything more than enjoy something. Participating in activities that bring joy will not only give back emotional real estate, but they also put us into a high state of mind to help energize us for whatever other challenges are on our plate.

MAKE YOURSELF AN OFFER

No dusty guitar? Not sure what could fuel your emotional real estate? One of my clients did something absolutely incredible, and I've since directed people to follow her lead.

Her typical Saturday would have involved a few loads of laundry, some grocery shopping, stopping at the dry cleaners, and hitting the bank. She would have gotten out of bed earlier, changed out of her pajamas, and battled an internal dialogue about all the things she should be getting done that day. In the past, she recognized, she would have taken care of more responsibilities, and she absolutely wouldn't have given herself permission to do anything fun because she always had something more important to get done.

Not this Saturday.

When she woke up, she made the conscious decision that she was only going to do things that gave her back emotional real estate. The whole day.

First, she brewed a big pot of coffee and sat on the porch

with her dog. That was her happy place, so she sat there in her pajamas until around eleven o'clock in the morning when she finally felt it was time to move. Then she did a bit of indulgent shopping, only looking at items that excited her—no shopping to replace her old nude colored briefs! She then came home to try a new yoga routine with some guided meditation and relaxation. She went upstairs, rolled out her yoga mat, and turned on the video. By now, her husband was curious about her strange behavior that day and poked his head in to question her. What in the world was she doing? After some playful teasing, she finally told him it was time to leave her alone so she could enjoy her practice.

He continued to pop up with questions throughout the day, but she carried on. That night, she made one of her favorite dinners, and instead of sitting in the TV room afterward, she tucked herself away in her favorite chair with a book that had been on her nightstand for months. By the end of that day, she said she felt so refreshed and felt she had gotten really clear about what activities felt good and what she could do to gain back emotional real estate. Finally, a vacation with no hours of travel delays or over-priced fruity cocktails.

When we take days—or even simple moments—to refuel with intention, we can also do them with priority and energy. When my student woke up that Saturday morning, her first thought was of ways to get that energy back. If she hadn't been mindful about her plan, she'd have probably ended up collapsed with the dogs at ten at night because she was exhausted from all that laundry, cooking, shopping, and unloading everything. Instead, she prioritized that time and came away energized and better able to handle those responsibilities that would normally have worn her out.

Even more impressive than actually taking the time to herself here is the intention with which she did it. She went all in, completely allowing herself to follow her instincts to create more space for herself. Because so much of emotional real estate is filled up with our mental dialogue, it's important to allow that time without pulling the double duty of thinking about bills, chores, and tasks that aren't getting done while we sit on the porch with a cup of coffee. Time giving back is time well spent—if you aren't truly committed to yourself in those moments, you won't be creating the space that you set out to create.

DESIGN YOUR OWN DAY

Thinking about your energy boosters, design your perfect afternoon, evening, day, or weekend—whatever you want it to be. Like my friend who spent her whole Saturday chasing what she enjoyed, use your list to create a day where you only do things that restore your energy.

Taking a day for yourself sounds delightful, but it's challenging for a lot of people to put into practice. Many of us fall prey to the message that we need to take on a self-improvement overhaul or it doesn't count—like we have to sign up for a meditation retreat, go to six yoga classes a week, and switch to a vegan diet—but what I'm talking about here is much simpler. Your perfect day doesn't have to be luxurious or expensive. Sometimes, for example, I just have to get my toenails painted.

When we're too busy to be happy, it's difficult to prioritize those moments. If cleaning out your email inbox feels like it's going to make you feel lighter at the end of the day, just do it. Or tackle a project that you've been procrastinating on. When I've spent two months tripping over the same boxes of clothes for Goodwill, and I know it only takes fifteen minutes in the car to drop them off, spending those fifteen minutes can give back massive amounts of emotional real estate. Give yourself space for that.

PASSION PROJECTS AND SIMPLE JOYS

What if you don't have the luxury of taking a Saturday to follow your bliss? What if you're struggling with extreme levels of burnout? It can be tempting to just change something—anything—to get some relief. This is why we put off big, rash decisions when we're low on the state of mind ladder.

One of my colleagues went through this. She'd left her job to stay home raising her kids, then ended up taking care of a sick parent as well. She didn't talk much about these things, though. Instead, she focused on challenges in her marriage. There was no abuse, no cheating, and no disloyalty—yet, somehow, leaving her marriage felt like a way out. It was the one change she was focused on making.

That didn't seem quite right to me. What I heard was a story of two very loving, very exhausted people who just didn't have a lot of space left for each other.

So, we started to talk about things that fire her up. Before she became a mom, she was an adventurer who loved to travel and do crazy things. Seriously. She would say things like, "If bungee jumping is involved, I'm there." *That* kind of adventure. None of what she described revealed a natural pull toward caregiving or nurturing. Left to her own devices, she never would have become a nurse or caretaker. She'd only become a caregiver because her family needed it and she knew it was important for someone to step into that role.

I didn't ask her to abandon that role, but I helped her look for things she could do completely for herself. When she would talk about her latest exercise classes, for example, she always lit up and became excited. Looking at it in that light led her to go for a Pilates teaching certificate. She loved studying the body and movement—just taking the courses had been enjoyable to her. When she received her certification, she began teaching out of her basement, and she loved it. Although her life got busier, teaching Pilates gave her back some emotional real estate and ultimately energy for her children and family.

She was passionate about it and was intellectually stimulated by her new adventure, which also happened to bring in some extra income. That financial flexibility allowed her to treat herself to lunch out on occasion without worrying about where the money was going. When she took moments like that, she gained some breathing room to reevaluate her marriage.

I checked in with her much later, and she said her marriage had never been better. She and her husband were going on vacations and had some fun stuff lined up for the summer. Everything felt like it had shifted back into place again.

It took some creativity to bring something back in that aligned with her intuition—to carve out some energy to bring something back into her life that she could enjoy. To bring her to a higher state of mind, which allowed her to connect with her husband from a higher state of mind. That shifted the marriage dynamic away from either one trying to make each other happy and into mutual reconnection, where two people both feel happy and work to connect. She shifted out of victim mentality and into ownership of her own role in the relationship as a whole person, rather than being interdependent and trapped within difficult circumstances.

Many people fail to prioritize things that are just for their own benefit, while keeping all their commitments to others. Nobody puts off taking their kid to daycare or picking them up, but the coffee date with your friend will be the first thing to go when a schedule feels too full. That's not to say that we shouldn't take care of our kids—but you likely know exactly the sort of thing I'm talking about.

The high-powered, professional men and women that I work with as a coach have an especially difficult time putting off conventionally responsible obligations to others in order to pursue conventionally frivolous things for themselves. While a passion project with great meaning, like teaching Pilates or playing guitar, can arguably be something that returns emotional real estate, it doesn't have to be. Rosa, from the beginning of the chapter, didn't need anything significant—just a calm coffee in the morning and a walk in the evening.

In reality, time spent investing in yourself and your emotional real estate is more than responsible and not at all frivolous. I've found that the people who give low priority to seemingly "non-value-added" pursuits are often the people who need the fun the most. I spend a good deal of time trying to convince these clients that although playing the guitar when you're not a rock star seems foolish at first—maybe you're not going to record a CD, maybe you're not even very good—it's still a worthwhile investment in yourself.

The best way to invest in more emotional real estate is to learn to recognize any tendency to ignore time for ourselves, then identify the things we can do to reclaim that time and move them up the list. Build them into daily life as a habit.

Keep your commitment to a Tuesday night golf game—not just one time, but consistently for six to eight weeks. Get into the habit of taking time for yourself, and you'll not only feel restored, but you'll find that the whole world doesn't fall apart when you let your guard down. The company isn't going to go bankrupt if you leave at 4:30 p.m. on a Tuesday. The kids are going to be fed, even if dinner's a little late. They'll still wake up the next morning happy and healthy, even if you took some time for yourself the night before. In fact, if you are happier, everyone might wake up happier and healthier—and arguably, more productive and wealthier.

PHOTO GALLERY

Another spin on the reenergizing list came from an interaction with a client who was struggling with depression.
She was burned out, and I was trying to help her reframe
her mindset a bit. She claimed to be too tired to take on a
new activity and felt completely disconnected from the
feeling of passion.

After some discussion, I challenged her to spend a few
hours that night out taking pictures of things that she
found beautiful. Taking photographs is a special way to
look at the world, because you have to become present
in order to take a picture—again, an approach to reverse
engineering mindfulness. It forces you to become aware
of everything around you and hunt for what you feel is
beautiful. Meanwhile, those other things on your mind
start to fade into the background for a bit while you focus
your attention.

She had once worked in architecture and happened to
love photography, so for the first time in a while, she was
up for the challenge. She started her adventure with a
picture of a latte that they poured for her at Starbucks.
She captured the milky froth suspended over the cup
and the powdered cinnamon she added for effect. She
captured an image of a charming neighborhood street
filled with tall mature trees. She snapped a photo of one
of her favorite buildings downtown that night lit up like

a Christmas tree, a cute café sign at one of her favorite shoe shops, and a portrait of the quirky people in the city, admiring the beauty of humanity. Afterward, she relayed how fantastic the practice was; she became connected with the pleasure of the present moment, a feeling she hadn't accessed in a long time.

SHORT-TERM WINS WITH LONG-TERM LOSSES

What I'm suggesting sounds intuitive—do the things you like to do—but remember that awareness is key. Not everything gives back.

For example, going out for a few drinks might relax you, so you feel like a couple of glasses of red wine each night will help you regain some emotional real estate. (This was a common practice of mine in my "stressed-out" days!) The problem is, habits like this can set in motion some unhelpful consequences. Your sleep may suffer, you might gain weight, and you'll probably feel lethargic during the day. When that happens, in spite of the quick break you feel you are getting from stress, you know you're drawing down your overall emotional real estate rather than restoring it.

Another common "treat" is food. Many of us have a sugar crutch; we often reach for that piece of chocolate or cookie that will get us through the day. Having a fresh cookie every afternoon at four may feel good in the moment, but if it interferes with your health goals and those pants keep shrinking in the dryer yet again, you might feel more discouraged and frustrated by your habit than comforted by it. You might use up a lot of emotional real estate berating yourself for giving in every day even though this "treat" isn't aligned with your goals.

And as I've mentioned before, social media is often a place where we go when we are relaxing...but it can sometimes create a feeling of energy depletion if we aren't mindful and disciplined with it.

Combine your instinct and self-awareness to create habits that support and refresh you by recognizing what feels good and thinking about the long-term impact. Instinct tells us what's rewarding right now; self-awareness lets us know if it's returning emotional real estate.

HELL YES!

In the spirit of finding things that energize us, I can't forget to pause to mention how making decisions that best suit us can also create energy. Decision-making eats up a lot of emotional real estate, but not deciding can eat up even more. If done right, however, great decisions can create a big return on investment.

I learned this little shortcut years ago when I was stuck on whether I should stay in a relationship. The coach that I was working with told me, "You know, I used to have a problem making decisions too, until someone told me this: it's either a *hell yes* or it's a *no*."

How do you know when you've hit on an idea that will give back emotional real estate? We tend to get anxious and procrastinate when making certain decisions. Say a job opportunity comes up, or you're looking at a house to buy, and you can't get clarity on the decision. You're stuck, and that uses a huge amount of emotional real estate. Your mind is busy weighing the pros and cons. *Maybe* if you take that job crunching numbers in the corner, it'll be worth it because it will help your career. *Maybe* the two-hour commute to the new house with the amazing kitchen would be worth it. You're just not sure.

I spoke with a woman facing this very dilemma. She deeply valued work-life balance and quality time at home, but then spent a long time considering a job that would require a longer commute and extended hours. She had some great reasons to take the job—better pay, more visibility—but it conflicted with the thing she valued most.

I asked her, "Is this your hell yes job?"

She immediately said, "I don't want to be stuck in traffic for two hours a day."

That job was not her hell yes. Even though she was disappointed, once she came to terms with that, she had a lot more clarity about what she was looking for.

So, do you hear yourself saying, "Hell yes"? A hell yes decision doesn't take a lot of time, energy, or emotional real estate. You know the answer. If I were to ask you if you want to go to the Bahamas next week, what's your answer? When I was asked to lead a women's retreat in Tuscany, it took me about 3.2 seconds to answer. "Do you want to go to Tuscany and lead a women's retreat in Debbie Travis's Tuscan villa?" *Hell yes!* I didn't ask a lot of questions. I didn't overanalyze it or talk myself into it, and I didn't feel anxious about my decision.

I've held onto hell yes decision-making since my coach shared it with me, because it was so vital for me at the time. Do you want to marry somebody who's not a hell yes? A good marriage, a good job, a good career choice, a good house—they're not going to flow from a lukewarm response, like, "Okay, maybe this will work—maybe if I just rationalize it more it will feel better." So, consider any big decision you might be trying to make by asking yourself, "Is it a hell yes, or is it a no for me?"

NO, FOR NOW

It can be incredibly hard to say no, even if something feels off. But we don't have to make all our decisions at one time. It's just the decision for now—and a "no, for now" doesn't have to be a no forever.

I've found that if it takes you thirty minutes to explain why it might be a good decision, you should try saying it's a "no, for now." I suggested this practice to a woman I know who was excited to move three hours out into the country, away from their suburban home. They drove out to look at the house, and though her husband continued to feel excited about the move, all of a sudden, she wasn't feeling it. The reality of that three-hour drive started to sink in. Her three children lived close to their current home, and she felt like they really needed her nearby.

The new house clearly wasn't a hell yes for her. But she wasn't sure it was a no, either. I asked her if she could picture it being a "no, for now." Maybe they needed to have a conversation about what a hell yes would look like for both of them, and whether they could align on that goal. Looking at it that way, they could open their minds to other opportunities. Who knows, they might find the perfect house only twenty minutes away, on a big open road with lots of land.

I can procrastinate and overanalyze with the best of them,

so I love using this framework for decision making. As I grow my awareness of what a hell yes feels like, making great decisions that ultimately align with my own feelings of "hell yes" can create a lot of energy for me.

BEST OF THE BEST, WORST OF THE WORST

Feeling you need more clarity? How about using this same "hell yes" and "no, for now" inspiration to design a fork in the road that feels right for you. I like to call this the BOB/WOW exercise, which is short for "Best of the Best, Worst of the Worst." It's a process I learned to generate solutions as a design engineer, but it applies to life as well.

For example, let's say you're making a career decision, but you can't figure out what's next. Call to mind all the jobs you've ever held—create a list as far back as you can remember. Now, for each job, make note of what were the *worst* parts of those jobs? The absolute worst of the worst. Everything that you couldn't stand. Now, capture what were the best parts of that job? The best of the best! Every factor, big and small, that made you enjoy or, for a brief moment in time, made you feel excited to be there.

Once you've created your list with your BOBs and WOWs, look for the themes and patterns that emerge. Did you love every job that let you work with kids, whether it was lifeguarding as a teen or teaching high school science? Did you hate filling out expense reports and processing piles of paperwork at every job you've ever held? (A pet peeve of my own!)

Each of those aspects tells you more about your instincts and what work energizes you and what depletes you. Once you get clear on that, start to think through the *next* decision you can make toward what you've learned, what energizes you. I call this the "Lily Pad Effect."

Imagine you're a little green frog sitting on a lily pad in a pond. Endless lily pads float around you, as far as your eye can see. You might want to examine them all, to determine the best path to shore, but you are overwhelmed then and immobilized to decide. But in reality, you can only look at the ones right next to you. If there are three lily pads you can easily hop over to—option A, option B, and option C—then all you need to decide on is which one will you choose for this first step. You don't need to know everything that will happen next, just pick the next best place to land.

Jumping back to your human body and brain, with emotional real estate waiting to be cleared, you need to simply pick a lily pad and start to make progress. Life is never going to be perfect, but if a choice feels intuitively wrong, it might simply be out of alignment with your authentic self. Sometimes we try to sell ourselves on one option, even though it doesn't feel right at a basic level. If you don't act on your no, you'll feel it; it will keep coming back around, taking up more and more emotional real estate. If you can gain some clarity about it being a no, you can avoid letting it become baggage that you'll carry into the future.

YOUR EMOTIONAL REAL ESTATE LISTING SERVICE

If we practice drawing our attention to these energizing options—like property listings for our emotional real estate—we can put them in play earlier, as soon as we're not feeling our best.

Not long ago, I hopped in my car to go to a doctor's appointment with my phone linked to my Bluetooth, and three of my favorite songs played, one after the other. As I started to hum along, and then sing and get totally absorbed into the lyrics, it reminded me of how much I love music, and it made me realize that I don't listen to music regularly anymore. Growing up, music was all around me. My family was musical, and I was a true Detroit kid who loved driving my car and rocking out to my favorite tunes. I had forgotten how much joy I can get from simply listening to great music in the car.

To keep this emotional real estate listing on hand, make

a list of events, activities, items, and people that give you lots of energy. You'll keep adding to this list all the time, sensitizing yourself to the things that spark joy. It's hard to remember the restorative power of rocking out to old Police tunes when you're in a moment of panic, but if it's on your list, you might just decide you need a little drive time during a bad day to help you revamp your emotional real estate.

What energizes others might not work for you or might not work all the time. Some people claim knitting calms them down, while others feel confused or agitated. Sometimes cooking gives back for me, and sometimes it doesn't. Nobody else can decide what goes on your list. Simply recognize the moments that give back. When you've captured your list, keep it available as a reminder of the things to try when your emotional real estate needs a boost.

Every piece of your emotional real estate is part of a system. Move one piece and everything else shifts. As you let certain things go and act on other things, you are working toward creating a life in a much more literal and feasible way. You're unraveling what balance actually means—not taking on a frustrating obligation that will tip the scales in one direction without moving something else off the scale. You don't have to maintain constant equilibrium but instead foster a continuing awareness that you can move things from one end to the other (and everywhere in-between) as needed. That's work-life wisdom, and you now have an extensive tool kit to accomplish it. There's just one more thing we need to cover, because not everything can be predicted in lists and exercises.

EXERCISE #7: RETURN ON EMOTIONAL REAL ESTATE

- Now we need to build an arsenal of ways to get more energy that we give. As we bring our focus to what creates a return on our energy investment, it will be easier to prioritize these things on a more regular basis.

- **A Hot Real Estate Day:** Visualize how you would spend an entire day if you were told you could only do things that give back emotional real estate to you. Plan out each part of your day. Each moment needs to be something that would energize you versus deplete you. (Hint: when you read your completed plan for the day, it should be such a "hell yes" for you that it's easy to agree you need to take action right away!)

- **Best of the Best Thinking:** If you have a big decision to make, consider creating a BOB/WOW list (best of the best/worst of the worst) to help jog your creativity. Use this exercise as a way to discover the themes and patterns that have either weighed you down or created more emotional real estate in your life.

- **Emotional Real Estate Investment Listing:** What does your emotional real estate listing look like? Can you create a list of thirty things that give you back more energy than they use? Stash this in a handy spot for future reference! (Yes, I say thirty items only because I want to challenge you to really brainstorm past the obvious things you are quick to reference. Think hard!)

CHAPTER NINE

When a Storm Rolls In

How do you survive a tsunami of grief? By being willing to experience it without resistance.

—ELIZABETH GILBERT

If you are like me, once you embrace some of these concepts, you'll find they are easy to follow. But this is life, and just when you've got yourself all sorted out, something will go completely sideways. A family member gets sick, your boss goes bankrupt, or a tornado takes out your house—suddenly, your carefully crafted world has started tumbling down around you. You might get laid off from a job, get divorced, or have a child diagnosed with a disability or illness.

A storm is anything that hits you out of left field and feels completely out of your control, and it can approach your valuable real estate from any direction. It can be so severe that it knocks old, deeply rooted trees down and crushes most of the colorful flowers you've planted and worked so hard to water. In the aftermath, things will look water-logged and bleak.

No one gets this "right" from the moment the storm hits until the sun comes out again. It's a storm, and that comes with all the chaos it implies. What you can do is recognize that you're going through a painful and upsetting experi-ence, and that it may take months before you can return to a new normal.

Shit is always going to hit the fan when you least expect it. Suddenly, unexpectedly, your world will get shaken up. It happens to us all at some point in our lives. You won't always have energy available in the moment of the storm. That's okay. Use these principles to help pick up the pieces when you're ready. Give yourself time to process what's happening. Give yourself plenty of permission to be angry, sad, scared, and pissed. Give yourself permission for things to get ugly while you weather a storm.

I can't tell you how to avoid life's storms, but if you're managing your emotional real estate well, you'll have the tools you need to reassert control even in situations that feel totally chaotic. Keeping this tool kit on hand is like winterizing your property—doing everything you can to prepare for the unexpected, from smaller unplanned expenses and burdens to massive life upheavals.

THE EYE OF THE STORM

It was a beautiful summer night, and I was hanging out with friends after an event at a golf course. The stars were bright in the clear, dark blue sky. Crickets chirped, and a band played into the night. I remember this moment so clearly—even thinking, *These are the moments we live for.* But that night, when I got home from the party, there was a voicemail from my dad waiting for me.

He said, "I don't care what time it is when you get this message—call me."

I took a deep breath and made that call. At midnight on a Saturday night, my father told me that my mom had been experiencing some odd symptoms, like slurring her speech, and her doctor had sent her in for an MRI scan. They never expected to find anything serious; they just wanted to check her for good measure. After the scan, she felt fine. She went power walking, got her nails done, and did some shopping. But when she got home, the hospital called and asked her to come in immediately to review her results.

The results shocked us all—my mom had a three-and-a-half by five-centimeter brain tumor. The doctors told us they were amazed that she was still walking and talking. Of course, she was admitted to the ICU on the spot with a plan to operate as quickly as possible. When the doctors determined the tumor was operable and not cancerous, they decided to do surgery within the week. And although this tumor needed urgent attention, this brain surgery was a risky one which could very easily permanently impair her memory and speech functions if it didn't go well.

My mom got to come home for a few days before the operation, and I was glad we got to spend some time together. Although I wanted to spend time worrying about what she would be like after the surgery, I used every ounce of energy I had to be present with her. She was right there with me and okay in that moment, and I wanted to experience every second of that—I had to consciously continue to choose to acknowledge that and not let my thoughts run too wild.

When the day of surgery arrived, we waited a long nine hours before we saw the surgeon's smiling face as he emerged from the OR. It was a complex operation—he had to unravel the tumor by microbits and detach it from her brain—but he felt great about the results. He cautioned us to not expect her to be able to talk for days after the surgery, but to our shock and delight, after surgery when we told her the surgery was a success, she whispered, "Great!" We were thrilled!

She spent some time in the ICU, healing slowly, but steadily. We were pretty amazed by how much progress she made in such a short period of time. None of the disasters I'd imagined had come true, and she was eventually allowed to go back home. With the crisis apparently averted, I went back to Toronto and got back to my business and clients.

It wasn't long, however, before I got another text from my dad: *I've got to take your mom back to the hospital. Something's wrong.* Mom had been taking a nap, and when my father went to check on her, she sat up and started vomiting. Within minutes, she was rushed to the hospital, and they sent her straight to the operating room. I threw a handful of things in a bag and jumped in the car to race back to Michigan, driving straight to the hospital.

This time, after hours of waiting through another marathon surgery, the surgeon came to us looking completely exhausted and defeated.

"I am so sorry. I don't know why this happened." he said. "Her brain started to bleed, causing a stroke. We just did what we could to try to keep her alive. We had to remove pieces of brain tissue and have no idea what the outcome will be. She could be rendered incapacitated—unable to walk or talk or remember anything. We really have no idea in a situation like this. Let's just hope for the best."

How do you process that kind of news?

We went home that night, sat around the table, and drank whiskey.

None of us had any idea what to expect on the other side of recovery. We knew Mom had survived, but would her personality come back? Would she remember us? It would be a long time before we would know, because her progress healing this time was much slower and very different. She wasn't moving. She wasn't talking to us. For a few days, she was in a coma state, her head bandaged, and eyes swollen. We simply sat with her, waiting for some change.

My mom not only was an amazing parent, but over my adult years she had become one of my best friends. I was devastated and overwhelmed, though I had enough presence of mind to remember what I'd learned about protecting and portioning my emotional real estate. Among the incredible sadness and worry, I tried to become conscious of saving my energy for the things that mattered most. While we waited for Mom to heal, I had to face the fact that other aspects of life simply had to go on the back burner for a while; I didn't have any emotional real estate available for anything else. I canceled as much work as I possibly could, and I don't remember socializing or attending any events. Instead, I got really clear on where I needed to focus my attention—managing my emotional real estate.

I tried to determine where I could add value or influence the situation. I couldn't control whether my mother was going to live or die or how she would heal, but I *could* become the patient advocate that she needed in the hospital. I could talk to her doctors and nurses. I could coordinate family members' schedules so that someone was always there for her. Feeling such incredibly deep sadness, I knew I would be able to help the most if I took care of myself along the way.

Each day, I had no choice but to refuel my emotional real estate, so I developed a very simple system. I would wake up early in the morning and get a really good cup of coffee before getting to the hospital the minute visiting hours began. I'd hang out there all day, while talking to family in person, on the phone, and via text about my mother's condition. Then every night, I would take a break from it all. I would go get my dog and run in a gorgeous park near my parents' house. For forty-five minutes, I'd listen to my favorite music and a let nature clear my mind and refuel my emotional real estate. As I ran, I would picture myself using up that pile of sadness as my fuel to keep me moving. I'd head to bed feeling absolutely exhausted, but my mind would be clear for just a moment and I'd sleep like a rock. I'd wake up feeling rested and do it all over again the next day.

VICTIMS OF THE STORM

The practice of emotional real estate has become so ingrained in the way I think, that as soon as I get into a serious fight-or-flight situation, I know I need to postpone anything that isn't urgent. I take care of the priorities that would cause me more problems later if I don't deal with them, but if a bill doesn't need to be paid to keep the lights on, or an appointment kept in order to keep my business open, I move it off my plate. Becoming fluent in the concepts of emotional real estate and using each tool in your kit regularly prepares you to use them subconsciously when things get really difficult.

While my mom was in the hospital, when I let myself get overwhelmed, I would slip into a victim mentality. *Why was this happening to us? How could this healthy woman be lying motionless in a hospital bed? Why are the doctors/ nurses doing things better or differently? Why don't they have more answers? Why didn't that doctor see this coming?* I had to make a conscious effort to hear those thoughts, see them as victim mentality, and then decide what additional, more empowering thoughts I needed to think. When those thoughts came, I had to recognize them, let them pass, and come back to an owner mindset.

What could I do that would help? When a storm hits, slipping into victim mentality is normal. Emotionally, you're at your lowest state of mind, and you have every reason to be. It's easy to feel overwhelmed by all the things outside of your control and dedicate a lot of emotional real estate to those things, but you don't have to.

When you're in the middle of a storm, the first thing you need to do is to reorganize your emotional real estate to make room for the bad weather. (Hint: notice how during 9/11 people who had years of grudges all of a sudden were hugging as they helped each other to safety? This is a simple example of where people, when thrown in the storm, no longer have the emotional real estate to keep feeding those grudges). Remember, you only have a fixed amount of emotional real estate that you can use to help influence it. Next, identify the areas where you do have some control and influence, and direct your emotional real estate into those things.

As my mother's healthcare advocate, I had to be her eyes and ears in the hospital, paying attention to everything about her care as if she were able to do so herself. I had to realize that my job wasn't to cater to the whole family or take care of seventeen other things—it was just to be her advocate. Some days, that meant something as simple as sitting at her bedside and feeding her macaroni and cheese. Other times, it meant conferring with a knowledgeable nurse. It wasn't my job to know whether she was going to live or what quality of life she might come back with. I was focused on the areas where I could create influence, and I let everything else go.

It wasn't easy, of course. Every time I would leave the hospital, I'd think, "Oh, my God, I'm going to miss something. What if she needs me?" Even though my dad and my brother made sure she was covered all the time, I wanted to be there twenty-four hours a day. I wanted to be there overnight. But given that I wanted to be of the most service possible, I made very clear boundaries about what I could physically do. Being there every hour of every day wasn't going to make me an excellent patient advocate. The way for me to make the biggest impact was to have energy and lots of hope, which meant I had to be in the healthiest state possible.

Sleeping and running were nonnegotiable. I always gave myself six or seven hours of sleep and a good cup of coffee in the morning, no guilt trips allowed. It did feel a little selfish when I had to turn friends down to save space to run or to spend some time thinking, but I did what I needed to do for me first. Other times, though, staying with a friend was just what I needed. I would go stay with one of my best friends, and we would laugh and talk about her life—not mine—and that soothed my soul. I had to give myself permission to have fun, even in the middle of the storm.

Like we hear in every single flight, we have to put our oxygen masks on before we can help with somebody else's. When you feel guilty about self-care, recognize that you're doing the right thing. You *have to* take care of yourself in order to keep fulfilling your responsibility.

WHEN THE STORM BECOMES A TSUNAMI

One of the first times my mom sat up after that second surgery, I walked into the room to find her looking completely confused. She seemed like she didn't even know I'd walked in. When she did look at me, I wasn't sure she recognized me. All of a sudden, I didn't feel strong anymore—this was it; my own mother looked right past me as if she didn't know who I was.

My stomach was in a knot, and I started to feel really weak. I couldn't breathe. For a couple of hours, I sat in the room, invisible to her. I cried—hard. I knew it was really bad. After I had cried all I could cry, I cleaned myself up and came back to my True North. Where do I have the power to influence anything about this situation? I looked for an empowering belief to focus on. Yes, she was incapacitated, but she was alive, and she was healing. And again, I need to stay focused on helping her heal to her fullest capacity possible.

A week later, during her hospital stay, she developed a fever. After watching her day after day, I had started to get used to knowing her movements and responses, even if she was not able to communicate. Just from watching her, something had changed, and I had a strong sense that her health was declining, and no one seemed to be listening. Doctors and nurses brushed me off and told me it was normal, and I kept challenging them as I really felt something was changing for the worse. After a day of really pushing the doctors and staff, I was supposed to go home for the night, and although she couldn't speak for herself, she looked like she was in pain, and her fever was still elevated slightly. My gut said something wasn't right. I decided I wasn't going home until I could release this nagging feeling.

I was angry at the hospital and felt that they were neglecting my mom. No one seemed to care that she wasn't quite right. It didn't feel like anyone was really paying close attention to her like I was. I wanted to rant about the failings of our healthcare system. Feeling exhausted, I could hear myself whining in victim mentality, which was not helping the situation. So, I decided it was time to shift into owner mentality. If I couldn't leave the hospital that night feeling good about her care, what else could I do? I was so frustrated and tired, it seemed nearly impossible, but if I *could* look at it from an owner mindset, what would I do?

I excused myself from her room and starting thinking. *What can I do? What can I do?* Then it came to me. She'd just been transferred from the ICU to a regular hospital floor. I went down to the ICU and found a nurse who had been competent and helpful and had cared for my mother just a few days earlier. I stopped him and asked for his help. I explained her symptoms and my concerns. I was careful not to accuse the nurses or doctors for not helping, because I wanted to encourage that nurse to think about solutions with me, not defend nursing practices.

I said, "If this were your mom, and this were the situation you were in, what would you do?"

He jumped in with answers. He walked me through exactly what he would do, and he helped me navigate not only how to get information and to get the right people to come examine her in an urgent way, but he also helped me to understand the politics of the hospital. He gave me so much information, I had to take notes to remember it all.

When I went back to her floor, I followed his instructions

exactly. I talked to the nurse manager and escalated a couple of the issues that I had seen, while being conscious to not rat out the hardworking nurses who'd been caring for her. By 11:30 p.m., we had five doctors in her room. They immediately did some blood tests and cultures and found a urinary tract infection had started to set in from days on the catheter. Before I left the hospital that night, Mom was on antibiotics to help her system start to fight the infection.

It was a small battle, not the war, but I went home feeling like I'd won. I went home knowing that I could pull off that sort of thing when I managed my energy right instead of feeling like I was a victim of everything she was up against.

A younger version of me might have gone home and cried, then stayed up all night worried sick about her. When they finally found the infection, I would have yelled at anybody who walked into her room about how terrible it was that they missed it—attempting to attack them through a guilt trip. The anger would have lingered, and I would have acted on the useless aspects of it. But displaced anger just places you at war with institutions. The problem with going to war with an industry or an institution is that you can't win. They're too big, and you're left with a giant grudge because there's nothing you can do. Instead, I knew how mindset and energy and the physics of emotional real estate worked. Instead of expecting my circumstances to change, I changed my strategy.

Often, my clients think that all the troublesome emotions will disappear when they learn to manage their emotional real estate. But storms still exist. They just don't hold you back anymore. The magic comes in that recognition—in paring down your emotional real estate to things you actually can affect regardless of what's happening around you.

Even though I was angry that I had to make it all happen, I also knew that was my role to do so. There was anger and sadness, fear and anxiety—all those emotions were real and present in the middle of this perfect storm. But it was my role to be her patient advocate, so I managed that energy very well.

EVERY STORM IS DIFFERENT

Over the autumn, my mother did heal slowly. She's back to almost 90 percent of what she'd been. She can walk, talk, and drive. Because she was a tax specialist, unfortunately, she was not able to go back to her old position. (My dad loved to tease the occupational therapists, assessing whether she could return to work by saying, "Would you let her do your taxes?") She stays busy exercising, cooking, quilting, taking care of herself, and chatting up a storm. She has plenty of memory to go around. While she still has health challenges and limitations as she works towards full recovery, she managed to conquer this storm. We all did.

Everyone's storms will be different in size, scope, and pain. Often, a loss of control can feel like a massive storm. It's common, when that happens, to slip into fight-or-flight. Your reptilian brain turns on and puts you in a highly reactive mode. In a way, this is the body's programming to free up emotional real estate so that it can focus on that giant stress storm. If you understand this response, you will recognize that some executive decision-making functions go by the wayside when a crisis hits.

Our ancestors would have gone into fight-or-flight mode when a physical danger approached. If a tiger was charging, it paid off to use all of their energy to manage their response. Yet we still react the same way. If your best friend is in a car accident, you won't be sleeping or eating well, and nothing will make sense—because your brain is shutting down those functions to direct most of your energy to fight or flee. Everything is devoted to coming up with the best response you can to that serious situation.

You might also notice that when things spin out of control, you long for power over *something*. Making big decisions seems like a way of regaining control, but that's not the way out. If you just found out your spouse was cheating on you, it's tempting to respond with brute force—like setting their car on fire or going on the hunt for the real person to blame. That's not always going to bring the answer that you want. Recognizing this lets you hit pause and gives you time to process the initial shock before trying to make a clear decision to move forward.

The bigger the storm, the bigger the decisions you'll have to make, so be careful. Time is your friend. On the other side of shock, you'll be able to make better decisions. You'll be more resourceful if you can give your body and mind space to process and then move forward. Take a little bit of time to manage your state of mind first, because your reaction in a low state of mind may not provide the best outcome for you in the long run.

TRICK YOUR BRAIN—DO THE OPPOSITE

Because your strengths and strategies are not mine and mine are not yours, the best way to prepare for life's inevitable storms is to look at how you've handled disruptions in the past. Do you turn and face them head on, or are you more likely to run for cover? Are you susceptible to taking on too much and burning out, or do you feel like folding the moment a crisis hits?

Remember, we don't analyze with judgment. Our patterns aren't good or bad—they are something to understand,

and that's the first step toward developing a new strategy for facing life's storms.

For example, one woman I know reacts to unexpected stress by not eating. It's her fight-or-flight response, and she knows that she's limiting her ability to react wisely by not fueling her body properly. She needs to eat, especially when she needs to make big decisions. Knowing that gives her something concrete to do when problems arise.

Her first step doesn't have to be a big one—she doesn't have to conquer a seemingly unconquerable problem in one fell swoop. She can start by drinking a smoothie or grabbing a handful of almonds. Something so simple can be powerful enough to trick her mind into thinking things aren't so bad. Do the opposite of what your brain expects during your stress response, and you'll trick it into thinking it can find a bit of calm.

I find that my first instinct when under stress is to cut out my workout to spend time and energy focused on the storm. Some days, I still do this, and I always seem to regret it. My favorite way to trick my brain is to hit "pause" and do a gentle workout for an hour to divert my attention to my body and my breath. It's hard for my brain to find the same level of worry or concern after having redirected energy for a short period.

REORGANIZE YOUR SPACE TO MAKE ROOM FOR THE STORM

Your first priority when a storm hits will be to reapportion your available emotional real estate. Something big is going to be claiming a lot of space, so what can you move out of the way for now? Think about the things you can do to free up your emotional real estate to focus on what's important right now.

When a client's husband broke his leg, for instance, she felt that a storm just arrived, and she worried how they would survive. She had a demanding job and two daughters, and she knew her husband was going to be out of commission for a while, dealing with pain, doctor appointments, rehabilitation, etc. She had so much on her plate already, and now this happened. As always, we don't get to choose when a storm rolls in.

We worked through a plan to shift some energy around. When she mapped out all her responsibilities, she realized she couldn't take it all on. Something had to give. She hired additional cleaning help at home, talked to her boss about moving some accounts onto an intern's plate temporarily, asked her mother to help out a bit more, and started doing her workouts at lunch instead of in the evenings. She worked her plan and commented that she went from feeling overwhelmed to feeling confident they were going to get through this challenging time.

With your emotional real estate shifted, next you can identify the things you can influence. A friend of mine who faced a series of invasive breast cancer surgeries recognized that she could influence her rest, her connection with her partner, her relationships with doctors, and her use of medications. She also decided that rather than let herself get depleted by the process, she could take people up on their generous offer to help. So, she recruited friends to deliver home-cooked meals to her, and asked people to sit with her and keep her company. It was important to her to have something to look forward to, so she started planning a trip for when treatments were all over.

We all wish we could prevent storms, but sometimes the best you can do is to see it coming and know you'll need a moment to build a strategy for weathering it. Even the worst storm feels more manageable if you walk in consciously deciding to manage your energy through the storm—it's like having a sump pump handy in case your basement floods; thanks to your advanced preparation, it's now a problem you can deal with rather than a disaster that sets you back permanently.

EXERCISE #8: WEATHER WATCH

This section is heavily focused for when the storms roll in. If you are thankfully not facing a storm, now is the time to waterproof your property. If you are mid-storm, reach for these practices to help you find that old dusty generator you tucked away in the basement.

- **Historical Weather Conditions:** Check in with yourself. How do you usually respond to storms in your life? Think back to previous storms. How did you manage your emotional real estate? How could you have managed your emotional real estate better in that situation? And finally, have you given yourself permission to let go of things that you could not control? Capture what you've learned.

- **Today's Weather Forecast:** If you feel a storm coming, get a piece of paper and draw a vertical line to make two columns with these headings: "Things that are out of my control" and "Things that are in my control." Spend time with this list, working to populate both sides. The more honest you are the better.

- **Let Go:** Give yourself permission to grieve what is out of your control. Give yourself permission to acknowledge that what is happening is different than what you wanted or expected to happen. Honor that. Allow yourself to use emotional real estate to process this.

- **Take Action:** Take action where you can. Find anything that you can do to influence the aspects of the situation that are in your control. Stay focused here when your energy allows for it. And remember, your reaction to any situation counts as something you can influence.

- **Free Space:** Find things that are less urgent that are using up emotional real estate, and see what you can postpone or put on the back burner for the time being.

Conclusion

It is our greatest responsibility to walk through life with intention and purpose. It means taking time to craft your thoughts, words, and actions with integrity. It means accountability. It requires self-inquiry. It is constant refinement. It is an ask for you to hold yourself into the highest regard. It is permission to shine.

—UNKNOWN

Five years after I gave my first speech on emotional real estate, people from the audience still find me and tell me, "I was so blown away by the concept of emotional real estate. Once you explained it, I couldn't un-see it."

Other people say things like, "Oh, my sister and I use the phrase 'emotional real estate' all the time now." It's becoming part of their language and the way they're talking about their energy and life.

That's how I knew this book had to be written.

I've since learned that if you want to become an expert on managing your emotional real estate, try writing a book about emotional real estate and just watch your existing stress levels soar (yup, I used the "S" word). Hitting "send" to get the last steps to publishing in motion is going to free up ten tons' worth of emotional real estate for me. But then again, when you're tuned into the things that are important to you, you can grow a business, write a book, and have a second baby all at once, if they're all important to you, and you are rigorous about how you manage your emotional real estate. Those three things were all big priorities for me, but I have to admit, other things had to take a back seat in the short term, and many other things got delegated to those around me.

There is a need in leadership and corporate culture for us to coach and support each other around emotional real estate. In fact, I've noticed a bias in many corporate environments *against* managing emotional real estate wisely. Sometimes, when a project is behind schedule or behind budget, leaders expect the team to *look* like they are using up all their emotional real estate on it in order to prove they're really on board. Other times, the leaders themselves model a stress-orientation that many of us automatically follow. The problem with both approaches is they exacerbate stress without actually improving performance.

Stress does not make people perform better or achieve more. Goals, commitment, accountability, and feeling supported do for sure. High stress might get people moving faster in the short term, but it is simply not sustainable in the long run.

I always encourage clients to create support groups with colleagues or with friends. Talk to your team or other leaders, maybe over lunch once a month. Start a book club, and work through the concepts and tools offered here. In part four, you'll find a guide that will help you do just that. Or simply get together over a glass of wine on Tuesday nights and hash it out; you'll find so many of us feel lighter if we can simply voice concerns and get them off our chest—off our emotional real estate.

Don't be afraid to train your kids on emotional real estate, either. Kids today often face packed schedules, bullying, constant social media input, and pressure from parents and teachers—a recipe for burnout.

When kids fall into a low state of mind, they often feel like it's going to last forever. I remember doing that as a teenager; one thing went wrong, and I piled on every other negative thing I could think of until the gloom seemed insurmountable. Remind your kids that their state of mind will change and help them find the first step in that direction.

You can also help them develop resilience by talking about things like taking action and letting go. If another child said something that made your kid feel bad, make room for those feelings, but also help them see what options they have in the situation. Can they take action on those things or let something go? How? Is there an empowering thought they can choose?

Most importantly, take care that your well-meaning actions as a parent don't actually pile more emotional real estate on your children. I know I absorbed the message from my parents that performing poorly—or not perfectly—in school was a huge disappointment. I went into every test feeling insecure, which is ironic because feeling stressed only lowers your state of mind and hampers your performance. It didn't help me learn the material on the tests; what I really learned was how to beat myself up repeatedly, because I didn't perform as well as I thought I should.

When we heal and find space to be happy for ourselves, we can increase emotional intelligence to help us better work with each other. If we were all armed with more awareness of emotional real estate, all our relationships and healthy boundary setting would be much more effective. We could notice each other's state of mind, the amount of free space they have, and what's happening in their lives.

This book was worth all the space it took up, because I'm doing this for you. I hope you're feeling much lighter now, too. Check in with yourself, now and always, and ask: are you happy? Are you moving toward happiness? Make that question the beginning and end point of your practice. Because you don't have to sacrifice happiness in order to live the life you've chosen.

If you've found value in these pages, you are more than welcome to reach out to me about how this fits into your personal life, your book club, or your corporate life. There could be value in bringing it into your company or into a retreat, and I would love to come work with you face-to face-in that capacity.

Emotional real estate should not be a secondary consideration, but a vital part of every decision-making process. Figure it into the equation. Balance it with time and money. Measure your relationships and other life pillars against your emotional real estate, because that piece— that will change the way that you think about *everything*.

I hope you've found the ideas in this book valuable and

the tools for practice useful. I hope you've enjoyed the read and found inspiration. But most of all, I hope you go on to think through these concepts all the time and begin to navigate things differently. So many times, we pick up a great book on meditation, stay in it for a week or two, then let it collect dust on a shelf.

I encourage you to make this more of a skill and practice than a topic in a book. I want you to create mastery instead of just comprehending an idea.

I hope it's a game-changer, because you deserve to be happy.

Part Four

Your Work- Life Wisdom Tool Kit

- Too Busy to Read This Book?
- Start a Revolution and a Book Club
- Quick Reference: Eight Practices to Expand Your Emotional Real Estate

Too Busy to Read This Book?

At this point, I imagine you're saying, "Yes, Christine, I understand what you're saying about emotional real estate, but what am I supposed to do next?" You might have read the whole book, or maybe you flipped back here in a desperate attempt to find something actionable—now! Maybe you're already overwhelmed, or thinking about the future, or trying to solve a relationship issue, and you want to put the ideas you've learned into practice, but it seems like a tall order.

The best—and maybe the only—way to make a lasting change is through practice.

First of all, if you have very little time, just read part two. By understanding the concepts of Emotional Real Estate (chapter three) and State of Mind (chapter four), you can dive in and create a practice for yourself immediately. Then, flip to Exercise #4, and get that Seven-Minute Morning built into your day. I can promise you this is the fastest way to get meaningful results from this book.

Then, keep this book handy for rainy days. I'm a big fan of practice, exercises, and tool kits. If you pick up this book and visit concepts and tools every time you feel incredibly overwhelmed, the practices will eventually become part of your regular problem-solving repertoire. If you can regularly guide your brain through a series of steps or processes, your brain will become used to following this practice each time things get stressful.

The exercises I've chosen for this book are high-impact and simple to implement. Many people assume there's a huge time commitment to managing stress levels, but that's not necessarily true. Practicing a new thought process can take as little as a minute; it's just that you'll need to do it again and again over time. Using these tools takes discipline, openness, and a willingness to completely engage with each practice.

Start a Revolution and a Book Club

Group work can be powerful. You might try it in a systematic way with a book club or a corporate support group. You could pull everyone in the office together to learn ways to motivate each other to reduce stress and feel happier, or you might try them out on your own and discuss them later. This book is divided into eight sets of exercises—this can easily be set out as monthly content for a book club discussion designed to stretch over eight to twelve months.

When I work with corporate leadership groups, I encourage participants to complete the exercises in full view of the others. When one person shows vulnerability, everyone else in the group feels less alone. They may also learn a number of new, interesting methods of coping with similar kinds of stress. Plus, when you talk about a challenge in the open, you pay attention; it gets clearly placed on your radar so that your subconscious mind can get to work on the problem.

One week, I might hear people I've paired up having an amazing conversation about emotional real estate, then the next week they'll come back with breakthroughs. "I finally stopped talking about it and went to check out the company's lunch yoga class. It was amazing! I felt so good that day." They'll take those action steps because the conversation placed it on their radar. When I lead these groups and work with women on these issues, they find those choices easier.

TIPS FOR WORKING IN A GROUP

You can access most of these tools on your own, but I have to admit I'm biased toward using a skilled facilitator to guide the study. There's never any harm in having meaningful conversations that could ultimately help us make better decisions about stress and burnout, but a solid structure can help keep you on track.

If you're a facilitator or group organizer, ask the questions listed in the study guide, then sit and listen without judgment. It's critical that you give space for people to think. The danger here is that, while your intention is to use this type of education to support friends, family, and colleagues, you might be tempted to act as the expert and problem-solver. Try to step out of the way and let them do that for themselves. Your role is to support. Let them have the experience that is best for them.

Ask people to open up and share, give them space for processing, and then share an observation. An observation is different than a recommendation. It might sound like, "As you're telling your story, I'm hearing that the morning feels more stressful for you than the afternoon. That's interesting. I hear you say that the fact your child got this teacher instead of that teacher makes you feel more stressed about the situation."

If the stressed mom just hears everyone in the group telling her what to do in the situation, she may feel judged and worried about the group's approval. The next time the group meets, she will probably feel like she has to explain what she did to solve her problem. She may fear rejection if she doesn't follow the group's advice. Now, there's one more expectation filling up her emotional real estate, and she doesn't feel supported at all. That's why understanding how to support people in their efforts to reduce stress is important. If we're not careful, we can add stress.

Eight Practices to Expand Your Emotional Real Estate

EXERCISE #1: MAP YOUR EMOTIONAL REAL ESTATE

One of the first steps to mastering your emotional real estate is to gain awareness of what you are using that energy on each day.

- **Step 1:** Ask yourself, "What is using up my emotional real estate right now?" List everything on your emotional real estate on a piece of paper and get it out of your head as fast as you can. Just when you think you've got them all, ask yourself, "What else?" Flush them, like a detox. All the thoughts that swirl around your mind over and over again, the things you can't stop thinking about—get all of those down. Put on some headphones, close your eyes, do whatever you need to do in order to dump them on a piece of paper. You can draw or list or doodle—whatever you need to do to visualize the thoughts, worries, plans, emotions, and concerns filling your mind.

- **Step 2:** Next, score each item from one to ten based on how much emotional real estate each item is using up. How urgent or intense are they? How often are they coming up? Give a ten to the situations that keep you up at night, the anxieties that consume every waking moment. Assign a one to problems that cross your mind every once in a while but don't seem like such a big deal. Other issues will fall somewhere in-between. Once you've listed all of the thoughts using your emotional real estate and given each a score, take a step back and look at what stands out. What's glaring at you, and does it surprise you? Is it interesting that you scored one above the other? The numbers aren't necessarily prioritization as much as observation and assessment.

- **Step 3:** Now ask, "What are my biggest priorities right now? If I were to better manage my emotional real estate, how would I be allocating it today?" Notice if you see a gap anywhere!

One thing to note: Often, when I have people draw or list the things on their emotional real estate, they get mad that silly things are taking up so much space. It's not uncommon to respond with, "That's it! I'm *not* going to use up so much emotional real estate on my mother-in-law's Christmas dinner demands ever again!" Enjoy the observation and don't feel the need to do anything right now. In later exercises, we're going to work on letting things go or taking action. For now, just be curious and grow as much awareness as possible so we can dive into more work ahead.

EXERCISE #2: SPOT OWNER MENTALITY AND STOP VICTIM MENTALITY

It's critical to grow awareness to when a thought is coming from victim mentality or owner mentality. It's easy to shift mindset when you can easily see where your thoughts are coming from.

- **Step 1:** When do you hear yourself thinking victim mentality thoughts? List as many examples as you can think of. (Hint: we all do this sometimes!) Examples:
  - I just don't have enough time. I can't get this done. It's her fault this is such a mess. If he wasn't so mean, we could be happier.
  - There's nothing I can do—guess I just have to put up with it. Nothing is going to change unless he/she/they change.

- **Step 2:** Where could you transition that victim mentality thought into an owner mentality thought?

Instead of focusing on the issue or what feels broken, try asking yourself, "What am I trying to create?" or "What would I like to see in the future?" or "What can I do to influence this situation?" Move your attention and focus from what is fixed to where you have influence. Finding where you are empowered in any situation helps you move up the state of mind ladder and really reduces the amount of space you feel something is taking up on your emotional real estate.

EXERCISE #3: MAP YOUR STATE OF MIND

It's critical to be able to visualize what state of mind looks like and quickly realize how it's influencing you in each situation.

- **Step 1:** Ask yourself: "When was the last time I felt like I was in a high state of mind? What circumstances put me there?" When you're in a high state of mind, what's going on? What's happening with your emotional real estate? How does this help you learn something?
- **Step 2:** What are some moments you can think of in which you were in a low state of mind? What was the quality of your thinking in those moments? What

were some of the thoughts you had when you were in that low state of mind?

· **Step 3:** Reaching for the empowering belief is one of the faster ways to shift state of mind. If I wanted to change my state of mind using an empowering belief, what empowering belief would I need to focus on in this situation?" (Example: I am strong. I am smart. I have the tools I need to do amazing in this situation. I know I will feel differently about this situation in a higher state of mind, etc.)

EXERCISE #4: THE SEVEN-MINUTE MORNING

You can make real changes to your emotional real estate and state of mind by starting with this short, simple practice. Plan five to seven minutes alone in the morning. Take your cup of coffee and hide in your favorite spot, like a reading chair. If the kids/dog/spouse/roommates are too distracting, book off the first fifteen minutes in your office. For example, I know that if I can get to my office with my coffee before 8:45 a.m., I'll have fifteen minutes to do my routine in peace and plan my day before my first calls start.

If you have to, you can get creative and do the routine on a commute, even on a train or on the subway. Talk through these ideas while you're driving using the voice memo app on your phone to capture your thoughts. It doesn't have to be on paper; all you need to do is to go through the thought process. I prefer to journal mine, but there's no wrong way to build this into your day.

It's about building something repeatable that you use over and over again to help you practice a new way of thinking about your day, your instincts, and your emotional real estate. Use your phone or a timer so you can fully immerse into the task without checking the time.

- **Minute 1: Silence.** In the first minute, get quiet. Become present. Don't look at your timer. This allows you to sit back, close your eyes, and have one full minute of silence. It will feel long but see if you can get comfortable with the quiet. Lengthen this as you build up some meditation muscles, but for today, one minute is all you need.
- **Minute 2: Moments to Savor.** Ask yourself: what are your highlights or favorite moments from the last twenty-four hours? When you bring a zoom lens to the best parts of your day each day, you start to enjoy those moments even more when they happen (you're thinking, "Oh *this* will be my best moment tomorrow during my seven-minute routine for sure!).
- **Minute 3: Emotional Real Estate Check.** Now that we are in a calm and high state of mind, what are the biggest things using up emotional real estate right now? What thoughts do I keep having? What

things am I worried about? Get those out on paper. Even exciting things can use up energy. Just jot down what's using your energy right now.

- **Minute 4: Empowering Belief.** Identify the empowering beliefs and affirmations that you need to remind yourself of today. For example: if you are worried about an issue with your spouse, you might decide "I am thankful for this person and I will choose to act out of love today" is your affirmation. If you are waiting to hear back on a big job, you might choose "I know my next great job is out there, whether it's this one or the next."

- **Minute 5: Envision Your Great Day.** Ask yourself, what will you do today to create more emotional real estate for yourself? And what would make today great? Not good, but great. For example, not just surviving a meeting but clearly getting your point across on a big issue. Or, not just having dinner with your kids but feeling like you really got quality time with them tonight. Visualize what that would look like. This practice can make the difference between having a wonderful day and simply surviving.

- **Minute 6: Action.** Think through any final thoughts on what actions you need to take today to make today great and feel you are managing your emotional real estate in an amazing way. Make a couple of notes about tasks that are on your mind or capture notes on ideas that bubble to the surface.

- **Minute 7: Brain Candy.** This last step is devoted to *brain candy*. Take a break to enjoy a quick clip from a book, a quick blog you enjoy, or to pick out a song that you need to listen to. Spend a second massaging in an essential oil to help revitalize your senses. Something that feels sweet to your brain—i.e., Brain Candy.

Some people do stretch this out into fifteen to twenty minutes, but be careful—the longer the routine, the less likely you are to do it every day. The magic here is in creating a habit that you build into your day that raises your state of mind and helps you gain clarity and insight into your emotional real estate.

EXERCISE #5: FIFTEEN WAYS TO LET GO

Now that we've become aware of negative thoughts that bombard your mind, it is time to let them go. Still, the concept of "letting go" can feel vague in practice. Here are fifteen practical ways to let go of something when you are convinced you can't. For this exercise, just choose one item you've been struggling with and apply one or more of these strategies to it. Write down the negative thought and explain why it's time to let it go, referencing any of the concepts below.

1. In a high state of mind, decide it's time to forgive

someone—either yourself or someone else. Do it because it gives back emotional real estate.

2. Notice if you had an expectation of a person or situation and not an agreement.

3. Contemplate how forgiving does not mean that you must condone or agree with what someone did—it means you are willing to free yourself and stop using emotional real estate to keep the story alive in your head of what they did wrong.

4. Find empathy for someone you feel judgment towards.

5. Let the universe work its magic—choose something that bothers you and make the conscious decision to leave it for something bigger to solve (Universe, God, Source, Spirit, Allah, Buddha, alien leaders from outer space).

6. Give yourself permission to never understand why something happened. See what that does for your emotional real estate.

7. See if you can find a situation in which you are using lots of judgment. Try to picture what questions a curious mind might ask about this situation.

8. List five reasons why this outcome could be exactly how life intended it to be and this experience is ultimately for your benefit.

9. Although something has upset you today, list five angry thoughts you have right now that you may one day choose to forget or let go of.

10. Play third person; pretend you don't know the whole

story. What pieces of the story could you be missing? Pretend you just learned something new. How would it change if there were pieces missing?

11. Honor the fact that each person is doing their best given what they are capable of, even if it doesn't match with what your best would be.

12. Choose an empowering thought to repeat to yourself right now. Find one that raises your state of mind.

13. Notice where your ego is damaged—remind your ego it doesn't have to be right or get its way all the time.

14. Be thankful for the whole experience of life, including the full range of experiences from joy to pain; as my grandfather once said, "You are just a spirit having a human experience."

15. Commit to fully loving the present moment, bringing all your attention to this exact moment—here is where you have control. Notice what each of your five senses are experiencing. Focus here. Now.

EXERCISE #6: LANDSCAPING TOOLS

Now it's time to bring focus to things we do over and over again that are not effective, and to bring attention to how we can create habits that actually serve us rather than hinder us.

- **Perfect System:** Ask yourself what action or belief you can change that would force the system to create different results. Can you draw a process map to show what belief drove an action that created the next belief and the next action? Do you see any flaws in your perfect system?

- **Create a Change of Habit:** Think of something currently sitting on your emotional real estate—maybe a habit of over-eating or sleeping in too late or leaving laundry in the washer overnight—something that just eats at your energy that you'd like to stop doing. Now think of the habit you want to create in place of that. For example, instead of drinking wine in the evenings, can tea take its place? Maybe you want to create a habit of doing the seven-minute routine each morning! Re-map the way that process looks, then take action. Hold your new habit constant for three weeks and see if your brain starts to re-wire itself.

EXERCISE #7: RETURN ON EMOTIONAL REAL ESTATE

Now we need to build an arsenal of ways to get more energy that we give. As we bring our focus on what creates a return on our energy investment, it will be easier to prioritize these things on a more regular basis.

- **A Hot Real Estate Day:** Visualize how you would spend an entire day if you were told you could only do things that give back emotional real estate to you. Plan out each part of your day. Each moment needs to be something that would energize you versus deplete you. (Hint: when you read your completed plan for the day, it should be such a "hell yes" for you that it's easy to agree you need to actually take action right away!)

- **Best of the Best Thinking:** If you have a big decision to make, consider creating a BOB/WOW list (best of the best/worst of the worst) to help jog your creativity. Use this exercise as a way to discover the themes and patterns that have either weighed you down or created more emotional real estate in your life.

- **Emotional Real Estate Investment Listing:** What does your emotional real estate listing look like? Can you create a list of thirty things that give you back more energy than they use? Stash this in a handy spot for future reference! (Yes, I say thirty items only because I want to challenge you to really brainstorm past the obvious things you are quick to reference. Think hard!)

EXERCISE #8: WEATHER WATCH

This section is heavily focused on when the storms roll in. If you are thankfully not facing a storm, now is the time to waterproof your property. If you are mid-storm, reach for these practices to help you find that old dusty generator you tucked away in the basement.

- **Historical Weather Conditions:** Check in with yourself. How do you usually respond to storms in your life? Think back to previous storms. How did you manage your emotional real estate? How could you have managed your emotional real estate better in that situation? And finally, have you given yourself permission to let go of things that you could not control? Capture what you've learned.

- **Today's Weather Forecast:** If you feel a storm coming, get a piece of paper and draw a vertical line to make two columns with these headings: "Things that are out of my control" and "Things that are in my control." Spend time with this list, working to populate both sides. The more honest you are, the better.
- **Let Go:** Give yourself permission to grieve what is out of your control. Give yourself permission to acknowledge that what is happening is different than what you wanted or expected to happen. Honor that. Allow yourself to use emotional real estate to process this.
- **Take Action:** Take action where you can. Find anything that you can do to influence the aspects of the situation that are in your control. Stay focused here when your energy allows for it. And remember, your reaction to any situation counts as something you can influence.
- **Free Space:** Find things that are less urgent that are using up emotional real estate and see what you can postpone or put on the back burner for the time being.

About the Author

Her Work: As founder and president of Leader in Motion, Christine is not only a coach, facilitator, public speaker, and consultant, she is an expert in change and ultimately an implementor. Her daily work includes time with executives and organizations, helping them re-think how they create a shift that drives lasting positive change. In 2012, she took on the role as executive director of the Women of Influence Advancement Centre and has played a key role in helping hundreds of female professionals advance their careers. She's worked extensively in sales organizations and with general management, and has delivered many engagements focused on culture change, diversity, and inclusion.

Clients: Christine has worked with numerous organizations in her career such as Vanguard Investments, Scotiabank, Vale, Samsung, KPMG, TD Canada Trust,

Sun Rich Fresh Foods, SureShot Dispensing, McCormick Foods, AmEx, SureWerx Safety, and PepsiCo. Christine is privileged to receive numerous invitations to deliver keynote speeches for a wide variety of companies and organizations. She has spoken at a number of conferences such as "Forward Together," "The Hope Symposium," and "The National Women's Show." Christine has also been featured as a subject matter expert regularly in *Women of Influence* magazine and has been featured in the *Globe and Mail*.

Credentials: She currently holds certifications in transformative coaching, neuro-linguistic programming (NLP), psychotherapy, and Miller Heiman business development processes, as well as a Six Sigma Black Belt certification focused on solving complex design issues. In over ten years as an entrepreneur and leader of the Women of Influence Advancement Centre, she's taught critical skills to thousands of professionals, and she's privately coached hundreds of men and women on creating their own career advancement.

Background: Christine started her career with an undergraduate and master's degree in mechanical engineering. After years as a design engineer, she joined a management consulting firm and gained further expertise on restructuring and implementing organizational change. In 2008, she made the bold decision to begin her own business. Today, her company helps numerous organizations improve workplace culture, implement coaching philosophies, and helps leaders operate at their maximum potential.

Connect with Christine to grow your work-life wisdom at:

- Website: www.myworklifewisdom.com (Sign up for our mailing list to get free tools, retreat dates, event dates, and find out how you can learn to lead, coach, and facilitate this work yourself. And NO, we won't send you thousands of emails or sell your email address to third parties—I promise!)
- LinkedIn: Freel free to reach out via an invite direct to Christine Laperriere
- Instagram: @myworklifewisdom
- Twitter: @myworklifewisdm (yes, sans the "o," since our handle was too long!)

Learn more about Leader in Motion at:

- Website: www.leaderinmotion.com
- LinkedIn, Facebook, Twitter & Instagram: Leader in Motion, @leaderinmotion